MEDIATION & ARBITRATION BY PATROL POLICE OFFICERS

Christopher Cooper, J.D., Ph.D.

University Press of America,® Inc.
Lanham • New York • Oxford

Copyright © 1999 by
University Press of America,® Inc.
4720 Boston Way
Lanham, Maryland 20706

12 Hid's Copse Rd.
Cumnor Hill, Oxford OX2 9JJ

British Library Cataloging in Publication Information Available

ISBN 0-7618-1368-3 (pbk: alk. ppr.)

⊖™ The paper used in this publication meets the minimum
requirements of American National Standard for Information
Sciences—Permanence of Paper for Printed Library Materials,
ANSI Z39.48—1984

TABLE OF CONTENTS

Note from the Author

At times, this book calls attention to the reluctance of police administrations and police officers to welcome nonconventional conflict/dispute resolution training and trainers into police work. Certainly, this phenomenon is problematic and one which must be addressed by conflict/dispute resolution professionals. However, having been a police officer, and being able to empathize with police officers, I assert that police officer skepticism of outsiders, in part, can be understood (although, it should not necessarily be condoned) by the lives which many police officers lead. The episodic nature of the work and the speed with which scenes begin and end, and the fact that many situations involving police are not seen in whole by those looking in, makes it difficult for some to understand many legitimate police responses.

It is important to note that analysis and scrutiny into many police actions is absolutely necessary and appropriate. However, it is also appropriate to acknowledge the work of good police officers and to realize that they too can be skeptical of outsiders, since even humane, legitimate, and appropriate police responses are sometimes not understood by those looking in.

CHAPTER 1
UNIFORMED PATROL POLICE OFFICERS

The uniformed patrol police officer is perhaps the most important member of a police department. Patrol officers are assigned to duties on foot patrol, or in scout or unit cars, wagons, scooters, bicycle, motorcycles, and horse-mounted. They are the police officers, street cops, who often represent the first government response to situations where there is interpersonal conflict and dispute. The patrol police officer's role in the interpersonal conflict resolution arena occurs frequently. Most of the patrol officer's challenges do not test his/her marksmanship or brute strength, but are challenges that test his/her wit, sophistication, analytical ability (including judgment), perceptiveness, and listening skills.

This book addresses the uniformed patrol officer and the interpersonal conflicts/disputes that he/she encounters on a regular basis while on patrol. It is directed at the uniformed patrol officer and to police administrators, policymakers, and dispute resolution professionals interested in methods that can improve the performance of patrol officers as well as better the delivery of patrol police services.

Within these pages are discussions regarding conflict/dispute resolution methodologies (or processes) for use by uniformed patrol police officers in addressing interpersonal conflicts/disputes. This book also provides the necessary information for police officers to employ these methodologies.[1] Use of these methodologies by patrol police can contribute to the following:

1. A level of professionalism on the part of the police officer and his/her department;
2. A decrease in citizen complaints against police;
3. A reduction in repeat calls-for-service, allowing scout cars and beat officers to be in-service[2] longer or responding to pressing emergencies;
4. Improved police-citizen relations;
5. A decrease in the need for use of physical force by patrol police officers;
6. An enabling for scene management (in a general sense, scene management occurs when a police scene is handled professionally and systematically).

Mediation and nonconventional arbitration, the focus of this book, are nonconventional conflict/dispute resolution methods. In patrol police-work, mediation and nonconventional arbitration can be pragmatically and effectively applied by police officers to accomplish patrol objectives. I describe these methods as nonconventional since they are not used in society as routinely as litigation and force to address interpersonal disputes.

Mediation can be defined as a neutral third party assisting disputants in resolving a conflict/dispute. Specifically, the neutral third party (e.g., the patrol police officer) is an active-assertive facilitator in the dispute resolution process. He/she does not impose a decision. Rather, he/she assists the disputants in fashioning their own agreement. The third party sets the stage for mediation by listening to the disputants, helping the disputants frame the issues, and keeping the mediation goal-directed in order that the disputants can fashion their own resolution.

Nonconventional arbitration can be defined as the intervention of a neutral third party (e.g., a police officer) into a dispute. The third party listens to both sides, and then, through a reasoned, logical process, he/she imposes a decision regarding the matter(s) of disagreement.

Take a moment and consider the common (conventional) methods of interpersonal dispute resolution used by uniformed patrol officers in their patrol duties:

1. Legitimate use of force (i.e., physical force; deadly force);
2. Arrest;
3. Coercion and or threats to arrest;
4. Avoidance (in reality, not a method but a response).

Avoidance represents a police response that is characterized by the police not doing what they are supposed to do or can do. Examples include:

1. When patrol officers arrive on a scene of an interpersonal dispute and do nothing pursuant to their discretionary authority, or omit to act in violation of their mandate;
2. When patrol officers make threats of arrest, or actually make a custodial arrest when arrest is not a legal alternative (e.g., situations in which everyone present is taken into custody, with police intent of sorting it out later at the station);
3. When patrol officers use illegitimate force (i.e., striking) or make threats to use illegitimate force (i.e., coercion by threat to strike);
4. Patrol officers disperse disputants (telling one disputant or even both to "take a walk") when police action such as arrest is warranted (i.e., in cases of domestic violence).

Conventional methods of dispute resolution by patrol police rightfully enjoy moments of legitimacy. To illustrate this point, let's focus on force for a minute. The police mandate is generally described in the context of police having a legitimate right to employ force.[3] Notwithstanding occurrences involving illegitimate use of force, there are times when force is used by police legitimately, however uneventful and or fatal (i.e., fatal shooting of a suspect). It is important to note that the ideas put forth in this book do not call for doing away with legitimate use of conventional methods by patrol officers. Rather, this book encourages the use of nonconventional methods as well as conventional methods.

Nonconventional conflict/dispute resolution (NCDR) methods/processes, for use by patrol officers, are those which do not involve force, coercion, or arrest. Mediation and nonconventional arbitration, two such NCDR processes, are suitable for use by patrol police officers in the following areas:

1. Public disputes;
2. Barricade situations;
3. Community-based disputes;
4. Domestic situations not involving violence;
5. Shooting scenes (e.g., the police come upon the body of a man shot to death in a robbery) in which disputes erupt between onlookers;
6. "Assist with property/clothing" (e.g., the scene may include one of the parties agreeing to leave a residential dwelling [or being required to leave pursuant to a restraining order or order of protection], and they seek to take/remove an item which the other party does not want to part with.);
7. Parent verses youth [runaway].

CHAPTER 2
METHODOLOGIES
MEDIATION

**(Note: Although the terms "dispute" and "conflict" have
distinct definitions, they are used interchangeably in the field of
dispute resolution. For this reason, the author has not
interrupted this practice in the pages that follow.)**

In the conflict/dispute resolution field, the term mediation can be defined as a neutral third party assisting disputants in resolving matters of disagreement between themselves. The mediator is an active-assertive facilitator, but he/she does not impose a decision. Rather, he/she assists the disputants in fashioning their own agreement. The mediator's role is that of setting the stage for mediation, listening to the disputants, helping the disputants frame the issues; and keeping the mediation goal-directed, in order that the parties can fashion their own resolution.

Mediation is often thought about as occurring in only an office. In fact, it might be assumed that the office environment is what creates the attention to necessary formalities of the process (e.g., only one person talks at a time). It would be prudent to abandon this notion. Formal mediation can be conducted by uniformed patrol officers on the street, in a bar, or on a basketball court among a multiplicity of venues.[4]

NOTE
A patrol officer can conduct mediation in a multiplicity
of places (basketball court; parking lot; living room;
or sidewalk). The process can be conducted where all
parties are standing up or sitting down.

The mediation process is a win-win process. When mediation is successful, all disputants end up winners, specifically because the disputants have fashioned their own agreement. Undeniably, there are times when a disputant leaves the process having accepted an agreement that offers less than what the individual most preferred. This does not mean that the disputant has lost. Win-win applies because each disputant agreed to the resolution and was an integral player in fashioning the resolution.

The patrol police officer by his/her very role in the community is sometimes unable to be neutral in community disputes; however, when conducting mediation, he/she must function as a neutral third party. Neutrality by the patrol officer during the practice of mediation is not a daunting or impossible task; it merely calls on the police officer to function as an objective professional.

Often, patrol police officers encounter disputes in which mediation is a viable method to resolve the dispute. In this regard, appropriate criteria for mediation by a patrol police officer should include:

1. The disputing parties are identified (and eventually available to partake in mediation);
2. At least two people are in dispute;[5]
3. The manifest dispute has not involved contemporaneous physical violence between the disputing parties;[6]
4. The disputants are willing participants in the mediation process.

Examples of disputes that are appropriate for mediation by patrol officers include property disputes, vendor-customer disputes, landlord-tenant disputes, and boyfriend-girlfriend disputes.

Let's take a moment and become familiar with some basic tenets. Disputes sometimes have two layers. The bottom layer is defined as the latent dispute (or underlying dispute) and the top layer is defined as the manifest dispute (see Illustration below). From this point on let's define the latent dispute as the underlying dispute.

We tend to describe the underlying dispute as that tension that we don't initially hear from the parties. In contrast, the manifest dispute is the tension that we hear loud and clear. The manifest dispute often results in shouting and sometimes physical contact between parties.

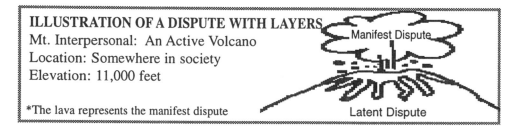

ILLUSTRATION OF A DISPUTE WITH LAYERS
Mt. Interpersonal: An Active Volcano
Location: Somewhere in society
Elevation: 11,000 feet

*The lava represents the manifest dispute

In most cases, we use the terms manifest and underlying in order to distinguish between two different levels of a dispute. The underlying dispute is typically the "real" matter in dispute. It can underlie the manifest dispute and propel it. Disputants are not always forthcoming with the underlying issues of a conflict (i.e., the latent dispute). The conflict resolution skills of the police officer will determine if he/she can facilitate in such a way that the underlying dispute is revealed (e.g., the officer asks the "right" probing questions).

When an interpersonal conflict has both a manifest and underlying dispute, the patrol officer can attempt to mediate both levels of the dispute. Of real importance may be the resolution of the underlying dispute. If the patrol officer is unable to mediate the underlying dispute, he/she may be able to mediate the manifest dispute and then make a referral to a community dispute resolution center where mediation of the underlying dispute will occur. The fact that the manifest dispute is mediated will make it less likely that there will be further immediate confrontation between the parties or a repeat call to the police. However, in some cases the manifest dispute is so strongly connected with the latent dispute that if both layers are not mediated, conflict will reoccur. The conflict could likely reoccur in the same tour of duty, hence, the police will have to be called back to the scene.

Again, when an officer is unable to assist the parties in resolving the underlying dispute, the mediation of the manifest dispute and a proper referral to the parties will make it less likely that there will be further immediate confrontation between the parties or a repeat call to the police. This outcome is called Conflict Management Mediation (CMM).[7] Utilizing CMM, the patrol officer mediates the manifest conflict or dispute in order to bring the dispute to a manageable level.

CMM is characterized as substantively handling (versus superficially handling) a police scene. All of the issues in the conflict may not have been addressed or resolved, but enough have been addressed or resolved that the disputants have entered into an agreement with the assistance of the officer. The police can describe the scene (or dispute) as mediated, under control and managed. Also, CMM can signify that the matters in contention (the underlying issues) have not been mediated, but that a truce has been arrived at via a mediation process. For example, the disputants agree to refrain from arguing with one another until such time that they make contact with the local dispute resolution center. Two other points are worth mentioning. First, CMM is appropriate for scenes on which police could mediate the underlying dispute, but they do not have the time. Second, perhaps, CMM also describes a process in which mediation was not conducted, but where the officer used his/her mediation skills to manage the scene.

The reality is, many disputes are extremely deep-rooted. Police officers cannot be expected to conduct mediations that every time resolve underlying issues (or even all the manifest issues in some disputes). Patrol police officers are not magicians. In many cases, outstanding nonconventional conflict/dispute resolution has been implemented, and good police work accomplished: (1) when the police are able to stop the shouting; (2) the manifest dispute has been resolved (or a truce entered into); and (3) the disputants are provided with an appropriate referral (i.e., to a neighborhood dispute resolution center).

Moreover, a referral by a patrol officer should not suggest that the patrol officer lacks conflict resolution expertise. Rather, there are occasions when the dispute would be best handled by another third party or agency. Typical agencies to which referrals are made include local conflict/dispute resolution centers and social service agencies (e.g., department of health and human services).

There are interpersonal disputes that do not have a bottom layer (or latent dispute). These types of disputes are defined as episodic. They represent confrontations occurring in a single event in time. This one-time event aspect, in addition to the fact that the disputants have not had contact prior to the dispute, can indicate an absence of underlying issues.

Mediation by patrol police officers is appropriate for disputes that are episodic in nature. Disputes of this type often do not involve a history or ongoing relationship between the parties. This often means there are no underlying issues in episodic disputes. The episodic nature of the dispute calls on the patrol officer to assist the parties in fashioning a resolution of the manifest matter. Examples of this type of mediation would include:

1. A dispute between picnickers (the parties do not know each other) over who has the right to a particular grassy area in a public park and neither party possesses a [special] permit;
2. A dispute over a parking space;
3. A dispute over use of a pool table in which the disputants do not know one another until the start of the dispute and will never have reason to see one another in the future.

Informal Mediation & Mediation Skills

There may be times when patrol police officers do not have the time to conduct formal mediation. In other cases, because of the nature of the scene (the scene is even more chaotic than normal), formal mediation is not possible, since it is difficult for the officer to adhere, precisely, to the steps/procedures of the formal mediation process. As an alternative, the officer can use informal mediation. Informal mediation represents mediation conducted in a systematic and logical manner, but without strict adherence to the steps of the mediation process (although the goal is still an agreement fashioned by the disputants).

Informal mediation can be helpful in certain disputes where if the officer took the time to recite the full explanation and opening statement of the mediation process, the fracas would quickly escalate. In other words, taking the time to define the process for the disputants, and then seeking oaths of voluntariness from each disputant could hinder the possibility of resolution. In these types of cases, the officer should use his/her common sense in deducing that the arguing parties would welcome the mediation process, then initiate mediation of the informal type.

Informal mediation can be conducted unbeknownst to the disputants. The basis of this method is that if the mediator can mediate a dispute without the approval of the disputants, the officer should mediate. Granted, the mediator has dispensed with asking the disputants to verbally state that they understand the process is voluntary. And certainly both informal mediation and conducting mediation unbeknownst to the disputants does not have to dispense with obtaining a verbal showing from the disputants that they want to partake in mediation. (For further discussion of conducting mediation unbeknownst to disputants, please see the section in this chapter entitled, Conducting Mediation Unbeknownst to the Disputants.)

Sometimes disputants lack the frame of mind to partake in the mediation process because of overwhelming panic, fear, or shock among other reasons. So, yes, there are times when formal or informal mediation by a patrol police officer may not be an alternative. However, let's keep in mind that even at chaotic scenes where panic and fear stricken individuals can be found, these scenes are not necessarily marked by disputants who lack the frame of mind to engage in mediation. Nor are these scenes necessarily inappropriate environments for officers to conduct mediation, especially, since these scenes are not necessarily characterized by decreased reasoning skills on the part of the patrol officer. Where there are sufficient units on a scene and time to mediate, the observations of this author pursuant to his field research and his own experiences as a patrol police officer, indicate that professional patrol police officers typically possess the ability to keep a cool head even on the most critical of scenes. All that is needed then are disputants who are willing participants and themselves cool-headed.

On those scenes when mediation is inappropriate, a patrol officer still has an advantage by virtue of having undergone mediation training. The officer's mediation skills bolster his/her arsenal of professional police responses. Perhaps mediation will not occur, but as a result of his/her mediation expertise, the officer will employ appropriate conflict resolution skills in order to calm, address the scene, and assist disputants in thinking rationally.

RULE

Always make sure to distinguish between mediation by the patrol officer of substantive issues (e.g., manifest and underlying issues) in contrast to mediation by the patrol officer of other issues in order to bring about a truce.

Employing Patrol Police Mediation

Mediation by patrol police officers is appropriate when the following phenomena exist:

1. An interpersonal dispute in progress, which comes to the attention of uniformed patrol police officers and which requires them to take some action.
2. An interpersonal dispute that has not come to the attention of uniformed patrol police officers, yet requires inquiry and intervention by the police.

Determine the Extent of the Dispute

When an officer is contemplating using mediation (at the outset preferably) he/she must determine:

1. The gravity of the dispute;
2. The likelihood of financial costs and losses to disputants;
3. The likelihood of legal (civil law) ramifications.

A high/significant level of any of the above requires that the officer not mediate the underlying issues. Perhaps a truce can be fashioned through a mediation process until a later time when other professional third party intervenors can become involved. However, when the underlying (or latent) dispute (not the manifest dispute) has a high level of gravity, a likelihood of significant financial costs or losses, or a likelihood of significant legal ramifications, mediation by the officers of the manifest dispute may still be possible.

When determining the gravity of the dispute, the officer must ask the question "How serious are the issues?" If the officer determines that the underlying issues are very serious (for example, if the parties need someone to assist them in resolving a will dispute, or if the parties want the officer to help them divide assets pursuant to a dissolution of a ten-year marriage), he/she should realize that a third party mediator (or other type of practitioner) with special expertise is needed.

Another indicator of seriousness is the presence of significant underlying issues. For example, when a daughter and mother are in dispute and the underlying issue is dissatisfaction by the adult daughter with the way that her mother raised her. Simply stated, there are times when the underlying issues are loaded with serious emotional and psychological baggage. The proper third party to assist in resolving this type of matter should be an appropriate professional with the requisite substantive expertise, as well as one who can devote extended attention to the dispute.

Financial costs and losses also influence the question of gravity. If what is being argued about/over is extremely valuable or expensive (e.g., who should have possession of a 70-year-old family heirloom), the officer should not mediate the dispute, but instead work on getting the dispute (the substantive issues) under control (scene management). He/she can do this with his/her mediation skills and a goal of CMM (Conflict Management Mediation).

Additionally, an officer should determine if the solution arrived at through mediation will necessitate formidable financial actions. He/she must determine if the resolution would place a party into a complex financial arrangement. If the answer is yes, to either the former or later, the officer should work towards getting the manifest dispute under control and subsequently making an appropriate referral.

Finally, in analyzing financial costs and losses, the likelihood of legal ramifications must be considered. For this category, the question the officer should ask himself/herself is "Does the matter in dispute raise significant civil law issues?[8] The key word here is significant (for example, the question of who is entitled to a piece of property; or what amount parties are entitled to as the result of a dissolution of a business partnership [where there is disagreement]). Once again, the officer should concentrate on managing the scene (getting the dispute under control) and referring the parties to other third party intervenors.

To review, disputes with a high gravity (especially if the issues are underlying), a likelihood of significant financial costs or losses, or a likelihood of significant legal ramifications should not be mediated by patrol police officers. Officers should concern themselves with managing the scene with other methodologies. If anything is to be mediated, it is those matters (not underlying issues) which enable a truce between the parties.

CAVEAT

"Return Disputes" are interpersonal disputes that, from an officer's analysis, indicate a high level of grave issues, a likelihood of significant financial costs or losses, or a likelihood of significant legal ramifications. Return disputes, if mediated, may "return" to the patrol officer because of questions about the validity of the agreement that the police officer assisted the parties in entering into.

> **RULE**
>
> For disputes with a high gravity, a likelihood of significant financial costs or losses, and/or likely significant legal (civil law) ramifications, patrol police officers should follow the following step-by-step process:
>
> 1. Officers should explain to disputants why they (police) cannot mediate the matters in contention (the substantive matters).
> 2. Officers should manage the dispute in order to bring about calm, perhaps using CMM (Conflict Management Mediation).
> 3. Officers should refer disputants to third parties (e.g., lawyers; local dispute resolution centers, etc.).

Determine the Type of Interpersonal Dispute

Once an officer has decided to try mediation on a scene, it is important that the officer try to determine if the dispute is episodic or part of an ongoing relationship. If the dispute is part of an ongoing relationship, the next question is whether there are underlying issues and if there are, whether or not they are moot? An example of a moot issue is seen in a dispute between two roommates who have decided to become ex-roommates. Each has made it clear that nothing in the world can keep them as roommates--they want to separate and not address underlying issues. They have concluded long ago that they are incompatible. The police have been summoned, since the roommates are arguing over who should take possession of the microwave oven. Upon arriving, the patrol officer learns that roommate 1 never liked roommate 2's mother. This matter of contention is likely moot since it does not bear directly on who takes possession of the microwave oven.

Another common example of an interpersonal dispute where the underlying issue is moot is the all too common "assist with clothing/property call," pursuant to an agreed severing of ties between boyfriend and girlfriend (and may relate to the issuance of a restraining or stay-away order). Considering the former, it's a boyfriend and girlfriend (roommates as well) that have decided to separate and simply want to address the issue of distribution of property (i.e., who gets the television). One of the parties has summoned the police for assistance in retrieving property from the former residence. The matter in controversy is property.[9] In the role of mediator, the patrol officer can assist the disputants in fashioning their own agreement as to which property is removed from the dwelling.

GENERAL RULE:

If the dispute involves an ongoing relationship or has a history, there may be both a manifest dispute and an underlying dispute. The officer's first inclination may be to try to mediate both the manifest and underlying dispute. The officer must listen for words which suggest that the underlying issues are moot, hence not in need of mediation.

GENERAL RULE:

Regarding whether the underlying issues are relevant. Notwithstanding the existence of underlying issues, if there is a reason why they are moot, then disregard everything except the manifest dispute. The disputants may fully acknowledge the underlying issues, but they want nothing more than the manifest dispute resolved, hence there is no use in dredging-up underlying issues.

Schematic of the Patrol Police Mediation Process

Step 1   Suggestion of Mediation & Opening Statement
Step 2   Each Side Conveys their Versions of the Events
Step 3   Reiteration by Patrol Officer of Key
          Points Conveyed by Each Side
Step 4   Brainstorming/Generating Possible Resolutions
Step 5   Agreement

NOTE
Mediation schematics are not etched in stone, they can always be altered.

> **ISSUE**
> It is common for patrol officers to talk with each disputing party individually before addressing both or all parties together. These one-on-one interviews/caucuses are particularly helpful in cases where one party is fearful of talking with the police in the presence of the other party. A patrol officer may not always find it necessary to employ this stratagem before beginning the mediation process. (This is a process that works smoothly when at least two officers are present, one to talk with each disputant).

Explanation of the Mediation Schematic
Step 1: Suggestion of Mediation and Opening Statement
    A. Introduction by officer if he has not already done so
    B. Suggestion of mediation (does not have to be profound)
    C. Explanation of the process (this statement may include an introduction of the process by name or simply its characteristics). Examples:
        1. Officer explains: "I will help the two of you reach a resolution."
        2. Officer explains: "If a resolution is reached it can be binding on you (the disputants)"
        3. Officer explains: "If a resolution is not reached, then I may have to impose a decision" (as in, to conduct arbitration).
    D. Officer recites "Ground Rules"

Let's consider each of Step 1's tasks individually:
A. Introduction by officer if he has not already done so
    If the officer did not introduce himself by name earlier, it is prudent, if possible, that he do so at this point.
B&C. Suggestion of mediation & explanation of the process (does not have to be profound)
    In suggesting mediation, the officer explains the process and highlights that participation is voluntary and that mediation is a win/win process in which the disputants fashion their own agreement with the officer's help. This is followed by the officer asking the disputants if they want to participate in the process.
    Example
    Officer says: "Okay folks, I can try to help you solve this prob-

lem through a process called mediation. Specifically, I want the two of you to work this out amongst yourselves--the two of you will decide how this dispute is resolved. My role as a third party is to facilitate[10] the process. I will not take sides, but I will help us all in understanding the issues and I'll make suggestions if necessary. If the two of you enter into an agreement, it will be binding, etc." (Explain how the agreement is legally binding in your jurisdiction). "This is a voluntary process, so if you decide not to participate or if you do participate and it does not solve the problem, then I may have to arbitrate the matter, which means that I will make a decision as to how this problem is resolved."

In this step, the officer would point out the benefits of mediation, particularly by calling attention to the drawbacks of other alternatives (e.g., arbitration takes the resolution out of the control of the disputants and civil litigation is a lengthy process).

There will be cases when an officer needs to adjust his/her vocabulary in explaining the mediation process to disputants. He/she must make the mediation process understandable (as a police method) to all disputants. Adjusting vocabulary is nothing new for patrol officers. Routinely, pursuant to social interaction, human beings adjust vocabulary to take into account the environment in which the interaction occurs, or to take into consideration the vocabulary of those with whom they are interacting. Simply stated, no one should make the mistake of assuming that mediation cannot be performed if one or both parties does not speak well, or lacks knowledge, education, or average intellectual ability.

ADVICE
It may be appropriate for the officer to explain the process without using the term mediation.

Following is an example of a brief opening statement in which the term mediation is not used:

Officer says: "I have a way that may resolve this dispute. In order for me to help, I need your cooperation. I am simply going to ask the two of you to work hard to come up with a solution to this problem. My role is that of keeping this process focused and helping the two of you fashion your own agreement." "Do I have your cooperation?"

In response to the officer's question, "Do I have your cooperation?" If the response is "yes" from both of the parties, the officer proceeds. If the response is "no," the officer can attempt to persuade the uninterested party or parties by stressing the benefits of mediation over another alternative. Patrol officers should not view all disputants who waive mediation as uncooperative People can have valid reasons for not wanting to partake in mediation. In many cases, a patrol officer should encourage a change of mind, but he/she must ultimately accept the decision of the disputant(s). When a disputant(s) chooses not to partake in mediation, the officer can still try mediation to bring about a truce (not mediation of the substantive issues). If this fails, nonconventional arbitration may be the most likely alternative.

D. Ground Rules

If the disputants agree to participate in the mediation process, the officer recites, very simply, ground rules to govern the process. Examples:
1. No profanity
2. No shouting
3. No striking
4. No interruptions
5. One person speaks at a time (Each party will have the opportunity to respond to everything that they have heard)
6. No threatening or intimidating
7. Agree to confidentiality (Confidentiality means that the matters discussed in the mediation session are not to be repeated by the officer or disputants to parties who do not have a legal right to the information. Because of the venues in which patrol officer mediation could occur, as well as mandatory internal reporting and documentation policies used by police departments, mediation by police officers may not offer the confidentiality guarantees which an external mediation center could offer. How much of the mediation is confidential and to what extent a police officer can invoke a mediator-client privilege rule are decisions left to the police administrators and policymakers in the official adoption of mediation as a part of scene protocols.
8. Although not exactly a ground rule, make sure to explain caucusing. Caucuses are one-on-one meetings between the officer and each disputant. They can be requested by the disputants or the officer. In caucuses, disputants can convey information to the officer that they feel uncomfortable discussing in the presence of the other disputant. (Caucuses are especially helpful when there are issues that one party is afraid to raise in the other party's presence.)

RULE
Adjust ground rules for the age, maturity level, and other characteristics associated with the disputants. For example, where the ground rule "no striking" is appropriate for many teenage disputants, it may not be appropriate for some adult disputants.

NOTE
The mediator may call for a caucus when one or both of the disputants continually violate the ground rules.

Step 2: Each side conveys their version of the events
- This is uninterrupted time
- One of the disputants is selected to speak first (may be determined by flip of a coin, etc.)
- Patrol officer(s) is actively listening and perhaps even taking notes
    Officer says: "I am going to ask each of you to tell your side, it's important that there be no interruptions when the other is speaking. Each of you will be given time to respond to anything that you disagree with or want to comment about. As each of you tell your side, I will listen carefully. After each of you has told your side, I will not impose a decision. I will simply help the two of you to fashion your own resolution."

Each of the disputants then presents their respective side. The officer only interjects when one of the ground rules is violated (e.g., interruption or use of profanity). At the conclusion of the second disputant's presentation, the officer returns to the first disputant and asks if he/she has anything else to say. The officer does the same with the other disputant. Participants use this time to rebut any assertion made by the other.

RULE
The mediator can call a caucus at anytime, as can either disputant. If the mediator/officer is outside standing on a sidewalk, and a caucus is necessary, he/she simply steps a few feet away with each disputant out of earshot of the other.

RULE
Rebuttals should not go on forever.

Step 3: Reiteration by Patrol Officer of Key Issue/s Conveyed by Each Side
- Officer clarifies (by reciting to the disputants) the key issues (e.g., first disputant wants second disputant to return his property; second disputant wants first disputant to stay off of his/her property).
- Officer asks disputants to verify that these are the issues.
- Officer encourages participants to agree, disagree, or modify the issues. Once there is agreement on the issues, the officer is just about ready to move onto the next step.
- Officer summarizes the issues amenable for mediation. He/she calls attention to issues not amenable to mediation.

Explanation: In some cases, a disputant(s) might not convey clearly what are the key issues. The officer has responsibility of sifting through information and finding, for the disputant(s), what are the key issues. In other words, the officer must possess the skill of issue spotting. The officer recaps the major issues in contention, aloud, and in an understandable manner for the benefit of both parties, as well as for his/her own clarification. She/he may do this by first reciting the issues raised by the first disputant, then those issues raised by the second disputant. The key points will involve what parties say they want or what they believe they are entitled to, deserve, or are owed (disputants should be encouraged to include reasons why). Note that it is also at this step that the officer must identify those issues not amenable to mediation. Having completed this task, the officer should ask each disputant if the issues have been identified. Disputants are invited to agree, disagree, or modify. The officer does not want to move on with the process until she/he and the disputants are all in agreement as to what are the key issues in the dispute.

It is also at this step that the officer may find that the substantive issues warrant referring the parties to a mediation center or other place (see section in this Chapter entitled, Determine the Extent of the Dispute). In this case, the officer should abandon the idea of mediating the substantive issues and mediate only those issues which will enable for a truce. The duration of the truce is the time period that disputants need in seeking and meeting with an appropriate third party intervenor.

> **CAVEAT**
>
> If the officer learns of child abuse, parental abuse or other alleged crime involving one of the disputants, for which he may not have an immediate criminal law alternative, the officer should not continue with the mediation process.

Step 4: Brainstorming/Generating Possible Resolutions
- Officer facilitates disputants brainstorming in an effort to generate solutions
- Officer listens for points of agreement
- Officer encourages dialogue on issues
- Officer holds caucuses if necessary
  (caucus may occur at this step, if necessary)
- Officer may want to suggest solutions

Explanation: The officer directs the disputants to brainstorm ideas in an effort to generate possible resolutions. The disputants rattle-off all of the possible resolutions that they can think of. The officer is the memory system for the process, hence he keeps a mental note of all of the suggestions. He further facilitates this step of the mediation process by helping the disputants to see all of the suggested resolutions clearly. He may even try to point out the benefits of each of the options/suggestions.

Even with many possible resolutions on the table, an impasse (the parties can't agree) is a possibility. Fortunately, there are ways for an officer to override an impasse (or attempt to override). First is by way of caucuses. Once again, a caucus is a meeting where the officer/mediator talks with each of the disputants individually. In the mediation process, a caucus is a way for disputants to convey matters that they don't want to talk about in the presence of the other disputant. Note that a disputant can call for a caucus. Even though only one disputant may ask for a caucus, when one asks, caucuses should occur with both disputants. Otherwise, the disputant not having a caucus might assume that the officer and other disputant are conspiring against him/her. For each caucus, if the process is held with all parties standing, the officer and disputant step several feet away (if held in an office, the caucus may be held in another room) while the other disputant waits until it is his/her turn to caucus with the officer.

The second tool for overriding an impasse is that of the officer returning to a previous step in the process, in some part (e.g., returning to Step 2: uninterrupted time; each disputant tells his version of events). Third, the officer could commence a new round of brainstorming, but this time the officer participates, he suggests possible resolutions (although, the officer must make sure that disputants fashion their own agreement).

The fourth method involves the officer reminding parties of the benefits of mediation. Emphasis is placed on the negative aspects of the alterative method (e.g., arbitration) to be used should the mediation prove unsuccessful.

It is at the **Brainstorming/Generating Possible Resolution's** step that the officer should be on the lookout for two possible pitfalls:[12]

1. **Irrational conceding:** These are situations when a disputant is not thinking rationally. For example, when one disputant asserts that the other can have whatever he/she wants and asserts, "Take all of the furniture and the house too!" Caution is advised, since these statements could be "heat of the moment" assertions. They may not reflect what the disputant really wants. Moreover, irrational offers and conceding may suggest that the mediation process is not the appropriate process, since disputants participating in mediation should be of sound mind.

2. **Power Imbalances:** Typically, these are situations in which one of the disputants is either intimidated by the other party and or has taken-on a subservient role to the other party. Here, one party usually has an advantage (e.g., emotional control). If the relationship between the parties is based on intimidation, mediation may not be appropriate. Just remember, the fact that one party is physically, or financially stronger, or more experienced in life than the other, does not necessarily indicate a power imbalance or that mediation is not an alternative.

ADVICE
When you encounter power imbalances and irrational conceding, perhaps a caucus with the perceived underdog disputant is necessary.

Step 5: Agreement
- Officer hears that there is an agreement. He/she repeats the agreement and, if necessary, states the agreement more clearly.
- If necessary, the officer should help in facilitating the agreement (e.g., how to implement a transfer of property).
- For some mediation agreements, excluding those that are episodic, a written agreement (and a copy for each party) is appropriate.

> **CAVEAT**
> Throughout the mediation process, the officer must listen carefully for a breakthrough (since the disputants may not notice). When he/she hears it, the officer should recap the agreement. If both parties are satisfied with the agreement, the officer may facilitate implementation of the agreement, i.e., the property is exchanged or given to another.

Normally, when a resolution is reached through mediation, a written agreement demonstrates the successful outcome of the conflict. When mediation is conducted by a patrol officer on a busy street, for example, a written agreement can be forgone if the officer decides in his/her best judgment that it is not necessary, and that the disputants are content without one. However, a written agreement does have specific benefits. The agreement can be a record of the action should the agreement be breached. In addition, the written agreement can be a reminder to the disputants, and perhaps better conveys to the disputants the binding nature of the resolution. Furthermore, for a variety of reasons, an agreement is less likely to be breached if it is written, signed, and a copy provided to each disputant.

Conducting Mediation Unbeknownst to the Disputants

On a scene, when an officer determines that mediation is appropriate, he/she should begin by asking disputants if they want to participate in the process. However, there are times when common sense can alert the officer that it is safe to assume that disputants want to participate in a mediation process. These are times when an officer will initiate and fully conduct mediation unbeknownst to the disputants and the term mediation is never mentioned. In many cases, conducting mediation unbeknownst to the disputants would be conducted contemporaneous with informal mediation. Note the following examples:

- The officer immediately requests that each party tell their side; or
- The officer acquiesces, when, upon his/her arrival, each party wastes no time in commencing an orderly delivery of their respective version of events.

In either case, after hearing both versions, the officer proceeds to Step 3 (Reiteration by Patrol Officer of Key Points Conveyed by Each Side). The officer summarizes the issues, and then moves to Step 4 (Brainstorming/Generating Possible Resolutions) by suggesting that the parties consider a variety of resolutions.

The officer always watches for infringement of mediation ground rules and alerts disputants to expected behaviors. Assuming that parties realize the expectations of the ground rules early, the mediation process can occur without the officer formally announcing expected behavior. Finally, if all goes well, a resolution/agreement is reached.

A Convincing Mediation Story

As a rookie policeman, I met a cop who was sharp, tough, courageous, empathetic, and the utmost of a professional. He respected his position and the citizens whom he served. Most important, although he had never undergone formal conflict/dispute resolution training, I learned that he was a brilliant dispute resolution practitioner. Not surprisingly, this officer was well liked by members of the community. He and I worked together on numerous occasions. We patrolled a busy, urban street. There were always people about in this heavily low to middle income Latino community which included a spattering of yuppies.

An event in which my colleague was involved illustrates the kind of patrol officer that he represented. On patrol one day, he entered a neighborhood store and suddenly found himself in the midst of a robbery in progress. He acted courageously in the face of a perpetrator who shot at him. The perpetrator missed, and the officer handled himself bravely and professionally in the ensuing gun battle, defending himself, the establishment, and stopping the perpetrator by shooting him.

Another example of my colleague's excellence occurred when I was a rookie officer. We were walking on a crowded sidewalk when two individuals approached us. They were involved in a customer-merchant dispute involving a piece of stereo equipment purchased within the past half-hour. The purchase was made from a merchant who operated a small variety shop. Outside the shop on the sidewalk, the merchant had a table set up from which some of the store's products were sold, and from where the customers had made the purchase that gave rise to the dispute. The customers wanted to return the item for a refund, since it was not exactly what they wanted. The merchant would not give a refund, so the two approached us for assistance as we walked our beat.

It was fall, early evening, and the street was bustling with after-work shoppers and folks heading home. I watched and learned as this officer mediated the dispute. To my knowledge, he did not have formal mediation training, yet he mediated the dispute like a "pro." He had each party explain their side, uninterrupted by the other. Then he looked for areas of agreement, then encouraged brainstorming. What began as a dispute involving an anxious customer and a merchant adamant about not allowing a refund, ended with a refund and both parties shaking hands and smiling. Best of all, there was satisfaction with the police involvement from the couple and the merchant.

A SCHEMATIC OF THE LAW ENFORCEMENT OFFICER MEDIATION PROCESS

Step 1: Suggestion of Mediation and/or Opening Statement

Setting the stage

- Definition of mediation: Mediator assists the disputing parties in fashioning an agreement; mediator does not impose a decision
- Introductions if parties not known
- Delivery of ground rules (e.g., one person speaks at a time; no profanity, etc.)
- Advising on confidentiality (what is said here will stay here; perhaps a confidential police record will be created)
- Binding nature of the agreement (e.g., what will follow if the agreement is breached)
- What will happen if mediation is not successful (e.g., arbitration may have to occur)
- Advise that caucuses may be necessary
- Negotiations must be done in good faith

Step 2: Each side conveys their versions of events

Uninterrupted Time (systematic manner in which parties are selected to speak). If there is more than one disputant on each side, no problem, one pair goes first then the other. Rebuttals follow the same process.

Regarding Rebuttals: only a reasonable number

Step 3: Reiteration by officer of key points conveyed by each side

- Officer clarifies (by reciting to the disputants) the key issues (e.g., first disputant wants second disputant to return his property; second disputant wants first disputant to stay off of his/her property).
- Officer asks disputants to verify that these are the issues.
- Officer encourages participants to agree, disagree, or modify the issues. Once there is agreement on the issues, the officer is just about ready to move onto the next step.
- Officer summarizes the issues amenable for mediation. He/she calls attention to issues not amenable to mediation.
- Officer has framed the issues, hence is keeping the process goal directed.

Step 4: Brainstorming/Generating Possible Resolutions

- Officer facilitates disputants brainstorming in an effort to generate solutions
- Each disputant has a turn to name all of the possible resolutions to resolving the dispute
- Officer listens for points of agreement
- Officer encourages dialogue on issues and possible resolutions
- Again, mediator listens for points of agreement
- Officer holds caucuses if necessary (caucus may occur at this step, if necessary)
- Officer may want to suggest solutions

Step 5: Agreement

- Mediator/officer specifies points of agreement as he/she understands them
- Officer asks disputants to indicate if the agreement, as the officer understands it, is accurate
- Maybe the agreement is memorialized in a written document (If written, try to write the agreement in disputant's own words.)

NONCONVENTIONAL ARBITRATION

The methodology arbitration is characterized by a neutral third party intervening into an interpersonal dispute, listening to both competing sides, then imposing a decision. In patrol police work, typically, arbitration is conducted by a patrol officer after the he/she has heard or learned of competing versions of an event. It is clear to the officer that one of the parties either has or does not have a legitimate claim to a piece of property or that he (the party) is or is not privileged a certain right (e.g., to remain in a specific location or to receive a service).

The arbitration process should be conducted in a systematic and professional manner: the neutral third party adheres to a step-by-step or methodological process; then makes a decision which is rationally based on the facts of the dispute. When arbitration is conducted in this systematic process, it's nonconventional (the term nonconventional represents that arbitration is not routinely conducted in this manner).

Arbitration of the conventional kind (e.g., not methodological or systematic) is used routinely by many patrol police officers in addressing interpersonal disputes. Its use represents a quagmire of decisions imposed without regard for the facts. The decisions are often the result of the officer not having actively listened; having half-listened; or an officer's indifference or lack of attention to duty. Even worse, when decisions are solidified with the officer's use of profanity and extreme threats. Poorly employed arbitration of this sort only leads to the dispute re-occurring. It is a sure recipe for a second dispatched call to the location, likely in the same tour of duty.

The premise here is that arbitration, when conducted properly, is in fact a systematic process. The idea is for cops to adhere to that process in decision making. Where in the officer's judgment (regarding an interpersonal dispute), he/she realizes that arbitration is the method to be employed, he/she should do the following:

(1) Gather all the facts (in some cases, this can occur within seconds) by having the disputants present their versions of events (either face-to-face or in caucuses with the officer).

(2) Based on the facts, he/she (patrol officer) uses his/her intellectual abilities, acquired academic and practical knowledge, and knowledge of legal and police procedures in deciding how to handle the matter, then imposes a decision.

(3) [The officer] Makes sure that after the decision has been made, that he/she can provide a rational, justifiable explanation for his/her decision.

Besides slip-shod use of arbitration by patrol police officers, it is used too often by many of them. For many officers, it is the only method they employ on scenes short of arrest for addressing interpersonal disputes. Considering this problem, it is a central objective of this book to convince patrol officers and police administrators that use of arbitration has its time and place in patrol police work. Officers should not neglect the other sensible methodologies (e.g., mediation) which are available to them to address interpersonal disputes and a variety of other types of calls-for-service.

Employing nonconventional arbitration requires active thought and listening by the patrol officer and that the he/she is cognizant that he/she is engaged in a systematic process.

Nonconventional arbitration has an objective of substantively (verses superficially) addressing scenes. Where either the manifest dispute or underlying issues are off limits to a police response (e.g., the matters are so grave, that to arbitrate them could have a high probability of significant civil law ramifications and/or potential for high financial costs or losses), systematic-nonconventional arbitration by the officer to effectuate a truce is recommended. For example, the officer does not arbitrate the substantive issues in contention, rather, he/she arbitrates those issues which are pertinent to bringing about a truce. In this way, the officers have managed the scene. The scene is still described as substantively handled, since any and all truces (or temporary compromises) should be followed by police referring disputants to those agencies that may be able to fully resolve or address the substantive matters.

RULE

Nonconventional arbitration should be conducted in a professional manner, to include sound discretion for selecting its use.

Nonconventional arbitration by a patrol officer can be a useful methodology when there is nothing to mediate. Examples:

1. The property in dispute clearly belongs to one of the parties. The best example may be that of a dispute in which a repossession "person" is dispatched by a bank to recover one of its automobiles (one to which the bank holds legal title). There is a dispute between the "repo man" and the owner of the vehicle, who attempts to impede the repossession process. The arriving patrol officer conducts nonconventional arbitration by:

   • Looking at the facts of the dispute by meticulously reviewing the repossession order;
   • If necessary, determining the legitimacy of papers, etc.;
   • Imposing a decision that enables the repossession person to carry-out the repossession.

2. The patrol officer arrives on the scene to find that a person is in possession of tangible property belonging to another. The taker admits to taking the property to satisfy a debt; however, the jurisdiction's law holds that the taking is unlawful. Here it is necessary for the officer to impose a decision.

Arbitration is appropriate when meditation has been attempted, but failed. For example, the officer has a mediation underway and the parties can't agree (impasse has occurred). He/she [the officer] has given the disputants ample opportunities to fashion their own resolution, including having informed the parties that he/she [the officer] would have to arbitrate if the parties did not fashion their own resolution.

There are other times when the mediation must be cut short to make room for arbitration. These are cases when facts are revealed in the mediation process which let the officer know that there aren't mediationable issues (e.g., remember the example involving the repossession man). Another situation in which the mediation is cut short occurs when there is a noticeable power imbalance or intimidation factor (e.g., disputant 1 is intimidated by disputant 2), so the officer must shift to systematic-nonconventional arbitration. Finally, but not least, parties may not be in the right frame of mind to engage in mediation; or they are, but decline to participate in a mediation process.

> **RULE**
> When the officer does not know if non-conventional arbitration is the appropriate approach, he/she may begin the dispute resolution process with mediation and then switch to nonconventional arbitration if necessary.

EMPLOYING THE PATROL POLICE ARBITRATION PROCESS

After an officer assesses an interpersonal dispute and believes that nonconventional arbitration is the method to be employed, he/she should do the following:

- Gather all the facts (in some cases, this can occur within seconds, although sometimes much more time is needed). The officer should encourage the disputants to present their sides.
- Based on the facts, the patrol officer uses his/her intellecttual abilities; acquired academic and practical knowledge; and knowledge of legal and police procedures in formulating and imposing a decision.

Description of the Patrol Police Arbitration Process

Instead of presenting a schematic of the patrol police nonconventional arbitration process as was done for the mediation process, it makes more sense to describe the nonconventional arbitration process in a less structured manner.

NOTE

A patrol officer can conduct the arbitration process in a multiplicity of places (basketball court; parking lot; livingroom; or sidewalk). The process can be conducted where all parties are standing up or sitting down.

The process begins in the same way that the mediation process begins. An opening statement is appropriate (e.g., ground rules are verbally articulated by the officer). This is followed by the patrol officer providing the disputants with uninterrupted time (each person has a chance to present their version of events). When the officer hears profanity or observes ill-courteous behavior, he/she reminds the appropriate party or parties to refrain from the behavior. Once the officer has heard both sides, he/she reiterates the issues to make sure that he and all parties understand and agree as to what are the issues--essentially, to make sure that everyone is on the "same channel." At this point, based on his/her analysis of the matter and consideration of applicable law and rules, and through a logical, systematic manner, the officer makes a decision which may mean that one party wins and the other loses or that neither party wins. A written understanding may or may not be necessary and is left to the judgment of the officer.

The officer may decide to let the parties know that if they disagree with his resolution, they may have other options (e.g., contacting a social service agency). Most important, the officer must be able to show that he/she arrived at her decision in a fair, systematic, and professional manner; and that the decision rationally based on the facts of the dispute.

WHEN IS THE RIGHT TIME FOR NONCONVENTIONAL ARBITRATION

- If there is a rule, law, or claim of right which gives the officer only one alternative, that of arbitration.
- If the officer can't use mediation, arbitration might be the next best approach.

Expediently Imposing Decisions

Although there is "informal mediation," there is actually no "informal arbitration." In most cases, decisions imposed by patrol police without a systematic process represent superficial and poor handling of a police scene. Exceptions which allow for expedient arbitrated decision-making by police in addressing interpersonal disputes include the following examples:

1. On the scene where an interpersonal dispute is occurring, there is a very severe, more pressing crisis which requires immediate police attention;
2. One of the parties is intoxicated, unavailable, or simply unable to partake in a formal nonconventional arbitration process;
3. The scene is too rowdy and perhaps dangerous to the officers. For their own safety they have to impose a decision and then leave immediately;
4. The officers must take immediate arrest action.

In hindsight, and if given all of the facts of the matter, an officer may assert how he/she would have handled the scene differently, but since one of the four variables above was present, the officer should not automatically be criticized for expediently imposing a decision.

MEDIATION & NONCONVENTIONAL ARBITRATION BY SHUTTLE RESOLUTION

Shuttle resolution is an avenue to conduct either mediation or nonconventional arbitration. Shuttle resolution is appropriate when all disputing parties, for one reason or another, are not on a scene, or the parties refuse to meet face to face. The officer addresses the dispute with mediation or nonconventional arbitration, but employs these processes by physically (to include telephonically) shuttling between the disputants. In the case of mediation, the officer/mediator conducts the full mediation process (adhering to all of the procedural steps), shuttling between the disputants and their respective locations. In other cases, the officer shuttles between rival groups as a mediator or arbitrator so to avert a physical confrontation between them. Note that many patrol police officers presently use shuttle resolution methods to handle calls-for-service, but in a less than systematic manner. Through conflict/dispute resolution training, police officers can learn how to conduct shuttle resolution in a systematic manner.

Employing Shuttle Resolution

Shuttle Resolution can be beneficial when a patrol officer learns of an interpersonal dispute where mediation might be appropriate, but the parties are not able to meet in the same room for such a process. The officer can function as a go-between. The officer simply moves between the parties with offers and counteroffers in an effort to resolve the dispute.

Shuttle resolution can be used to resolve a dispute between two rival groups of teenagers that have been involved in an ongoing dispute with each other. The officer would go to the first group (to the leaders of the group if not the entire group). She/he would explain the mediation process (see the mediation schematic process in this chapter), and ask the group to participate. If the group responds yes, but will not meet with the other group face-to-face, then the officer can mediate by shuttling between the disputants. Other options include:

1. Mediation conducted unbeknownst to the disputants;
2. A hybrid of shuttle mediation and "mediation conducted unbeknownst to the disputants;"
3. Nonconventional arbitration;
4. Conventional approaches.

If shuttle resolution is the selected approach, the officer will shuttle in an attempt to get agreement on at least some of the key issues. Shuttle resolution can also be a start to getting the parties to mediate face-to-face.

RECONCILIATION AS AN OBJECTIVE OF PATROL POLICE MEDIATION & ARBITRATION

The term reconciliation defines a process of establishing a friendship or partnership as well as reconnecting a broken relationship (e.g., business partnership, recreational friendship, etc.). With regard to patrol police work, in some cases, officers can mediate disputes with the objective reconciliation. This is done by the officer assisting the parties not only to resolve their dispute, but also to re-establish a friendship or to continue a business arrangement, etc.

TO REMEMBER

Mediation is amenable to reconciliation as an objective. The officer can help the parties mediate a resolution that re-establishes the relationship of the disputants or builds a relationship between the disputants.

Mediated agreements/resolutions without reconciliation are sound and 100% legitimate. Although it would be nice if all mediated agreements included reconciling between parties, the reality is, this is an imperfect world and an overwhelming amount of mediated disputes will lack reconciliation.

When a patrol officer convenes a mediation with the objective of reconciliation, it is in the interest of keeping a managed or resolved dispute from causing a subsequent police response, as well as creating harmony within a particular setting or community. To illustrate the point, consider the many situations when reconciliation should be attempted by the officer because of the structure of the relationship of the disputants/parties. For example, the disputants are roommates, neighbors, family living in the same household, or they are work-mates. These are situations/structures where the parties must continue a physically, close-by existence after the police leave. Reconciliation between the parties, therefore, seems like a sensible objective for the patrol officer to pursue.

A NOTE OF WISDOM

Patrol officer mediation that includes reconciliation benefits positive social interaction in the world in which we live.

Schematic of the Police Reconciliation Process

(Note: In addition to being described as a methodology, reconciliation can also be described as the type of outcome sought.)

• The officer decides to employ mediation or nonconventional arbitration with an objective of reconciliation.

In the mediation process, at the point when the officer assists the parties in brainstorming for possible resolutions, the officer makes suggestions and encourages the parties to re-establish their relationship. The officer may remind the parties that before the dispute they (the disputants) were friends or business partners or that they are sisters, and reside in the same home, etc. The officer discusses the importance of resolving the dispute and resuming their positive relationship. If the parties work or live side-by-side (e.g., they are neighbors), the officer conveys how that very fact necessitates reconciliation. Following is an example of what an officer would say to disputants in attempting to re-establish a relationship between the disputants:

Officer: "I can see that the two of you are good friends-right?"

Hopefully, the parties will nod yes or respond yes.

Officer: "I sense that both of you want to continue being friends."

Hopefully, the parties will nod yes or respond yes.

Officer: "Let me help the two of you get your friendship back on track."

Reconciliation may not have its best results when used with patrol officer nonconventional arbitration, since in nonconventional arbitration the officer imposes a decision that may not be popular with one of the disputants. However, it is possible that the officer can point out to the non-victorious disputant how and why the nonconventional arbitration was equitable (or in the disputant's best interest) and maybe then the disputant would be open to the officer's attempts to have the parties reconciliate.

POLICE SCENE CHARACTERISTICS AND PHENOMENA OF INTERPERSONAL DISPUTES

1. Sometimes in interpersonal disputes, both of the disputants are present and sometimes one disputant has left the scene;
2. Sometimes a crime is committed for which the police must take arrest action (e.g., a scene where, because one or both of the disputants are taken into custodial custody, the situation is not amenable to mediation or nonconventional arbitration);
3. Sometimes patrol police officers are radio dispatched to an interpersonal dispute;
4. Sometimes, while engaged in patrol, officers stumble upon the scene of an interpersonal dispute;
5. Sometimes, while engaged in patrol, officers are flagged down or approached by citizens who report an interpersonal dispute that they have witnessed or are themselves involved.

In the above list, the most important characteristic is that sometimes one disputant has left the scene and only one of the disputing parties is present when the patrol officers arrive. In cases other than when the dispute is episodic (e.g., the disputants will not likely ever meet again), the officer may want to seek out the other disputant. The officer can determine if this is necessary by considering:

1. The severity of the dispute;
2. What if any damage would occur if the dispute were handled unilaterally;
3. The geographic distance (proximity) from the scene to the location of the other disputant.

As a general rule (if the officer realizes that the disputant is within his/her precinct or near-by), in order to prevent escalation of the dispute as well as a possible repeat call (concerning the dispute) to 911 within the same patrol shift, the officer should seek out the other disputant.

There are cases when bringing the disputants face-to-face could escalate the conflict. These are cases when shuttle resolution should be considered. The telephone is helpful in this regard. The officer simply moves between the parties with offers and counter-offers in an effort to resolve the dispute.

There will be times when the officer, in his/her best judgment, decides against trying to resolve the dispute. Instead, the officer may refer the present disputant to an outside agency or advise the disputant of alternative courses of action (e.g., file a court action or notify another public agency).

————————— **Exercise 1** —————————

For one minute, think about an interpersonal dispute in which you were involved in your role as a patrol police officer. At the onset of the scene, there were no grounds for the arrest of either or any of the disputants. Another officer on the scene overreacted unnecessarily. His/her actions escalated the scene. (Perhaps, a physical confrontation ensued or a person was taken to jail, or both). You were angry at the other officer. His/her "John Wayne" actions may have, or did cause harm to you and other officers, as well as could have, or did result in a reprimand for all of the officers present.

For one additional minute, think about how you could have handled that dispute using mediation, nonconventional arbitration or another method that would not have escalated the scene.

————————— **Exercise 2** —————————

Assume that as you patrol your beat, the newly appointed director of a neighborhood advisory board approaches you. She tells you that she has heard about the police using mediation on interpersonal dispute scenes. If she asks why mediation is an approach worthwhile to patrol officers, what would you say? Either on paper or in a role-play, explain how you would describe the process to the director and what benefits you would tell her the process has for disputants.

This exercise can also be staged as a role-play in which the officer has been invited to address a community group. He or she is standing in front of a large audience of people and has the task of showing audience members why patrol police mediation makes sense.

THINGS THAT THE PATROL OFFICER MUST CONSIDER IN EMPLOYING MEDIATION

First and foremost, patrol officers must acknowledge and accept that interpersonal disputes are normal, healthy, and in some cases productive. After all, disputes enable us to take note of a problem. If an officer thinks that only "bad" people become involved in interpersonal disputes, then it is necessary that he/she correct that notion or select another profession. It is very important that police officers address interpersonal disputes with the understanding that conflict is an important and necessary part of life.

Upon arrival, patrol officers should assess the scene. If the officers determine that one or both of the disputing parties is not to be taken into custody or that the interpersonal dispute at hand does not involve violence of the type for which the law mandates that police must make a custodial arrest (e.g., two men who are pushing each other as the police arrive--they are about to fight) the officer should consider using mediation as an alternative.

Following is a list of considerations for police officers to rely in determining whether or not a nonconventional conflict/dispute resolution methodology such as mediation is an appropriate response to an interpersonal dispute scene.

1. The Applicable Law
A. What does the legislation, for example, mandate for this type of scene? Is there a law that supersedes the use of mediation? If there is, then the officer must adhere to the tenets of the law.
B. If the law enables discretion, then the officer should briefly investigate the scene so to determine if the scene is amenable to mediation.

2. Applicable Administrative Policies or Rules
Are there absolute rules that mandate how a scene must be handled? If there are, the officer must adhere to the policy or rules. If there aren't and the officer has discretion, then mediation may make sense.

3. Environmental & Social Context
A. Consider: disputants culture; cultural phenomena in general; and the social setting and geographic venue in which the dispute is occurring.
B. Think about how people in the community in which the scene is located perceive the police. If there is often mistrust or fear of the police, then any effort to make use of mediation must include making the parties feel comfortable and confident with the mediator/officer.

4. Other Parties or Entities
A. Determine if the interpersonal dispute transcends the scene. For example, are there other parties or entities not present which have valuable input into

how the matter is resolved? Do the present disputing parties have the authority to fashion their own agreement?

B. If the officer determines that there is some other entity or party (or even an external rule) that has an interest in how the matter is resolved, mediation of the substantive issues is not a likely alternative. An alternative could be Conflict Management Mediation (CMM). CMM enables for handling the scene using police officer mediation skills (e.g., via mediating a truce). (See CMM previously in this chapter)

5. **Objective Standards**
   For example, with regard to a property dispute, what do the parties assert that the property in contention is worth (e.g., the blue-book value)?

6. **Possible Solutions**
   Relative to the scene, does it appear that mediation can enable for solutions which satisfy the expectations of each of the disputants? If the answer is yes, then mediation makes sense.

7. **Other Issues**
   Once an officer has decided to use mediation, he/she should consider how he/she will handle the scene if mediation does not work.

SOME GENERAL CONFLICT/DISPUTE RESOLUTION SKILLS FOR PATROL POLICE OFFICERS

What are the skills that a patrol police officer must have in order to employ mediation, nonconventional arbitration, and other nonconventional conflict/dispute resolution (NCDR) methodologies? Below is a list of some of the most important skills (These skills are necessary once the NCDR process is underway).

1. **Listening** The officer must be an active listener.
2. **Issue Spotting** (Identifying Key Issues) By being a good listener, the officer is able to spot the relevant issues. Try this exercise so to see why listening is so important: Remember Jane, Dick, and Spot. Okay--let's focus on the canine Spot. Please repeat the name Spot five times. Let's begin: 1. "Spot" 2. "Spot" 3. "Spot" 4. "Spot" 5. "Spot"--What do you do when you come to a red light?_____[13]
3. **Articulating the Issues** The officer is able to articulate the issues in his/her own mind. This enables for his/her full understanding of the matter(s) in disagreement and enables the officer to facilitate a process that focuses on the issues rather than extraneous matters. For example, if nonconventional arbitration is the selected method, being able to articulate the issues enables the officer to make a logical decision. At some point it may be necessary for the

officer to recite the issues and frame them for the disputants in order that everyone is on the same channel.

4. **For the Officer's Benefit Especially-Transforming a Raw Dispute into a Manageable Form** When officers encounter a dispute, sometimes people are shouting and the issues are all over the place. By transforming the dispute into something manageable, the officers do away with people shouting, as well as help the parties frame the issues and bring the dispute into perspective.

5. **Not Showing Favoritism to One of the Parties** A patrol officer wants to avoid being perceived as favoring one disputant or position over the other. This rule applies especially to mediation. One way that an officer can avoid accusations by disputants that he/she is playing favorites is to make sure that where he/she is sitting or standing is equal distance from each disputant and that his/her eye contact with each is equal. Officers should choose their words wisely in responding to compliments from disputants during the mediation. Some disputants may be sincere in this regard, while others will be manipulative. Finally, officers should refrain from gestures such as nodding yes or sounding words such as "I see" or "I see your point," etc. These words and gestures might cause one disputant to believe that the officer is playing favorites.

6. **Identifying and Articulating Areas of Agreement** Irrespective of the method employed, the officer should listen for points/areas on which the disputants agree, then bring the points/areas of agreement to the attention of the disputants. In the case of mediation, this practice will bring the parties closer to a resolution. In the case of nonconventional arbitration, this practice will enable the officer to logically and justly impose a decision.

7. **Since beginning a sentence with "you" sometimes has an accusatory tone to it, try to use "I" rather than "you"** when addressing some disputants. Remember though, that just putting an "I" in front of a your statement is not necessarily sufficient. If the I-statement focuses on the other person's faults, it is likely no different from a you statement. Essentially, I-statements should express what the officer needs to have happen (i.e., "I need people to step back"); or an I-statement can express the officer's concerns about a situation (i.e., "I think that this dispute needs to mediated in order that this situation does not become worse, etc.).

8. **Be cognizant of the symbols that your body language sends.** Your stance or facial expressions may escalate a dispute. If you are wearing sunglasses and a disputant is not, perhaps you will be perceived as indifferent and aloof. Also, try to be cognizant of what the body language of the disputants is conveying.

9. **Try to not to assume or use stereotypes** in assessing disputants.

10. **Don't make statements which back people into a corner.** When you make these statements, you are asking for a fight. For example, any statement that is socially unacceptable; or one that typically incurs an intense wrath from the hearer Examples include, statements about an individual's mother or statements about an individual's race, ethnicity, or sexual orientation. When you make the mistake of causing a person to believe in his/her own mind that you have invaded sacred ground; or when you make him/her feel, in his/her own mind, that he/she has lost face or been humiliated (especially, if the incident occurs around his/her friends or family) you escalate the situation greatly.

11. **Remember that when some people are involved in an interpersonal dispute, they scream, curse, and behave dramatically.** Let them vent--don't take it personally--Very seldom is their aggression or anger directed at you. If you take a moment and let them vent, they will calm down in most cases.

ROLE PLAYS

Below are 9 role-plays heard on real calls handled by police officers. These role-plays are designed for patrol police officers to partake in as actors. Videotaping role-plays can be a valuable learning tool.

REMEMBER

NCDR MEANS NONCONVENTIONAL CONFLICT/ DISPUTE RESOLUTION. Mediation and nonconventional arbitration are [types of] nonconventional conflict/dispute resolution methodologies.

The role-plays have the following benefits:
1. To make NCDR training fun, exciting, and not boring.
2. Through role plays, officers can try-out the mediation and nonconventional arbitration skills that they have learned (especially, in an effort to perfect the skills).
3. Role-plays enable all watching and participating to realize the benefit of NCDR methods and skills in accomplishing police patrol objectives.

Trainers, when conducting a training, use a camcorder to film role plays. Following the film making, put the cassette into a VCR so that all in attendance can enjoy the playback. This can create laughter and an overall congenial atmosphere, even when a critique of the film (with input from officers) is underway. If you are a police administrator or contracted trainer, don't leave home for a police NCDR training without a camcorder.

Note that these role-plays can be modified and now and then should be. Furthermore, I intentionally left fact gaps in the role-plays. This is where the creativity of the trainer and actors is needed and welcomed.

Role Play #1

You and your partner are dispatched to a scene where you find two adult siblings quarreling over two cordless telephones, both of which are owned by them equally. One of the siblings has hidden the receivers. The other sibling wants one or both of the receivers returned in order that he/she can make a telephone call. The sibling who has hidden the receivers exclaims that he/she has hidden them, since the other is always occupying what is the sole telephone line in the apartment, thereby making it difficult, for him/her to make telephone calls. *Role players, try mediation.

Role Play #2

Devon and Casey have purchased a walkman from a neighborhood, licensed, sidewalk vendor. They had set out to purchase a walkman with an "auto-reverse" feature. Unfortunately, after purchasing the walkman and inspecting it, they realize that it does not have auto-reverse. They quickly return to the merchant, explain their dilemma and ask that the vendor provide them with a refund. The vendor refuses to offer a refund and Devon and Casey ask two uniformed officers (on a foot beat or assigned to a unit car) for assistance in the matter. The disputants were not given a receipt (as is routinely the case when an individual purchases from a sidewalk vendor). Granted, the disputants can bring a small claims court action, but let's assume that they would appreciate it if the patrol officers could try to handle the situation.
*Role players, try mediation, etc.

Role Play #3

Ms. Dobson is the homeowner of a home at 3005 15th Street. She owns an automobile and always parks it in her driveway. The driveway is large enough to accommodate one vehicle. When her grown children come to visit, they can park their vehicles in front of their mother's house, on the public street, provided there are spaces available. Often, there aren't spaces available, since the neighbors, Mr. and Ms. Powell, who live across the street, don't use their driveway, which accommodates three automobiles; rather, they park at least two of their three cars in front of Ms. Dobson's house. (The reason(s) why the Powell's don't use their driveway is up to your creativity.) Ms. Dobson's grown children are left with having to park at another location on the street that is farther down the street but in walking distance of their mother's home. Ms. Dobson is unhappy that her children cannot park in front of her house. Ms. Dobson and the Powells' have been neighbors for the past 27 years. In the past two years, each side has summoned the police at least six times regarding this matter. You and your partner have not responded before. Assume that each and every past call was legitimate, but that the dispute was not substantively handled by the other units. *Role players, try mediation, etc.

Role Play #4

You are walking your foot beat (or you are in your unit car) when you are approached by a citizen. In a respectful and clam manner, she begins to tell you an account of how she and her boyfriend have just broken-up. You realize that she is a drug-addict and lives on the street as does her former boyfriend. She explains that the former boyfriend refuses to allow her to have her portable tape-radio player, worth about ten dollars. You accompany the woman to the makeshift home in a nearby alley. The former boyfriend is present and is very cooperative. Both he and the former girlfriend are willing to participate in mediation in order to resolve the dispute. The girl-friend asserts that she purchased the radio, he asserts that she may have paid for the radio, but that in the relationship that had lasted several months, he most often earned money for the relationship via the collection and sale of recyclable soda-cans. *Role Players, try mediation

Role Play #5

It is a cold winter night, you and your partner receive a radio run described by the dispatcher as an "assist with property." You arrive to find that the situation involves an unmarried couple that after 7 years has decided to separate. In the past couple of days, the boyfriend has removed all of his belongings to his new apartment, but there is an issue over two remaining items, a coat and SONY Trinitron television (one of the two televisions in the apartment, the other is an RCA--neither party has a receipt for the television--except for different brand names, both televisions are practically identical, of equal value and quality). The male is ready to leave the apartment, but he wants to take the television that he claims he purchased. The girlfriend agrees that he purchased the television, but has other reasons for wanting to keep it for herself (use your creativity in determining what those reasons are). The boyfriend also wants to take a coat that he bought for his girlfriend for her birthday only days ago. You and your partner arrive to find a civil couple. In fact, they are disagreeing amicably — not shouting or behaving erratically. Early on in the mediation process, the male throws-up his hands and announces that he will leave without the television, but wants the coat. He puts on the too small, flowery ladies coat. Your first inclination is to chuckle, since he is now laughing and the girlfriend is uncontrollably laughing. Perhaps there is hope for this relationship.

*As are most of the role plays, this one is based on a call that I handled. How would you handle this dispute? Try resolution by mediation with reconciliation as an end. This role-play can also be tried out in a variety of other ways: e.g., arbitration where mediation fails.

Role Play #6

You are on the midnight tour of duty. You receive a radio run described by the dispatcher as "an injured person." You arrive to find calm, but also a man is bleeding profusely from a severe gash. He is holding his forearm in place. If he lets go, it may detach from his arm. You radio for an ambulance if one is not already on its way (considering the seriousness of what you see, even if you know one is on its way, you would likely ask the dispatcher for an ETA and inform him/her of just how bad things are). You and your partner learn that the injured person is the husband of the woman who is standing a few feet from you. The married couple shares the apartment with the mother of the injured party. It turns out that the injured party voluntarily and deliberately put his hand through a window to display aggression in an argument with his wife. The ambulance arrives and transports the injured party to the hospital. You follow in order to have the necessary information for your report. Outside of the hospital room in which the injured party is being attended to by physicians, you attempt to obtain more information for your report from both the mother of the man and the wife/daughter-in-law. They become involved in a heated argument in which the mother blames the wife for causing the son to put his hand through the window. Mother and wife are not in violation of the law (although, they could be approaching violation of a disorderly conduct statute). Using mediation, or your mediation skills, or other nonconventional skills, you as a patrol officer should try to:
• Calm the parties;
• Obtain the information that you need;
• Make it possible for both parties to go home peaceably.
    (Note: You have bungled things if the matter escalates as a result of your intervention style)
*This scene, like the others, is based on an actual scene.

The three role-plays that follow do not involve an interpersonal dispute. These exercises are intended to illustrate how NCDR skills (in particular, mediation skills) are great resources for patrol officers in handling a variety of matters, even those not involving an interpersonal dispute (in which the office is a third party intervenor).

Role Play #7

A couple is visiting your jurisdiction from Denmark. In Denmark, it is routine, accepted, and legal for parents to park a baby carriage (think of the traditional 4-wheel baby carriage), in which their infant child rests comfortably, outside of a restaurant window as the parents have lunch, dinner, etc. The visiting couple does not take note of cultural differences, hence, in the manner described above, they park the carriage holding their infant child outside of a restaurant as they have a meal inside. One of the many people who pass by and notice the carriage contact you and your partner. (Would it matter if the couple was having Margaritas?)

*Those individuals playing the infant's parents should present themselves as either arrogant (i.e., they are not phased by U.S. law and culture); or unable to understand what the "big deal" is all about.

Note: In New York City, in the Spring of 1997, the police became involved in an event similar in character to this one.

Role Play #8

A great-grandmother, 81 years-old to be exact, who walks with a cane and has problems seeing and hearing is visiting her son, his wife, and their children for the Thanksgiving holiday. While visiting, the grandchildren give their grandmother a puppy. At the conclusion of the holiday, the grandmother who is too frail to travel by air, is taken to the Greyhound Bus station where she boards a bus for a six-hour journey. Approximately four hours into the journey, the puppy who was resting comfortably inside the woman's large shoulder-bag, awakens and makes canine noises. In the middle of the late night/early morning, at a gas station in the middle of nowhere (an extremely rural and desolate area), the driver orders the woman off the bus and commences to recite that the bus company policies forbid animals on its buses. Assume that you are in your unit car at the gas station and you observe and are in earshot as the woman is instructed to remove herself from the bus. Assuming that the woman has been removed from the bus, but the bus has not yet left, if you intervened, how would you handle the situation using mediation and other conflict resolution skills? Assume that you have an opportunity to talk with the bus driver.

Note: An event almost exactly like this one occurred in November 1997. The police shuttled the woman home, via collaborations by a variety of police departments. A unit car in each department took the woman as far as each jurisdiction would allow (to the municipality's limits), then where the cruiser in the next jurisdiction would take the woman on board and the process would start all over again until she was home.

Role Play #9

You and you partner are directed by the dispatcher to respond to a block in which gun shots have been fired. Upon entering the block, you notice a man laying on the sidewalk in a pool of blood. He is in a semi-conscious state with two bullet wounds to the abdomen and one to the head. You go to him and kneel by his side. Your partner takes the car and initiates a canvass for the shooter. The individual sounds several words, then dies. Seconds later, as you are kneeling over the body, you learn from a reliable source that the deceased was a 3rd year medical student and is now dead as the result of a robbery. He was shot when he did not turn over his wallet fast enough. Soon additional units arrive. The scene is cordoned off. The task of collecting shell casings and other evidence is underway. The brother of the shot individual arrives to the scene and wants to go to the body of his brother. He confronts you and an air tight perimeter of police officers responsible for keeping people away from the body (so to preserve the crime scene). Assume that you don't know that he is the brother of the deceased until he tells you. Assume that he is so distraught and traumatized that he may not be very articulate. Assume that he is loud, boisterous, and overcome with emotion. How do you handle this matter without escalating the scene? Use your mediation skills as well as other nonconventional conflict/dispute resolution skills.

CHAPTER 3
MANDATING MEDIATION, NONCONVENTIONAL ARBITRATION & OTHER NCDR APPROACHES IN YOUR POLICE DEPARTMENT

Perhaps after reading the preceding chapters you believe that mediation and nonconventional arbitration represent sensible ways to accomplish patrol objectives. The question is how to officially incorporate these methods into patrol police response protocol? Attempts to introduce and implement these methods and others like it in many U.S. police departments will no doubt be contravened and stymied by primarily six factors:

1. Limits on the amount of time that an officer is permitted on an assignment, i.e., time constraints on calls-for-service mandated by police department policy.

2. Police departments which do not require that officers satisfy adequate educational standards that, if required, would better assure that officers could learn how to implement modern patrol officer tasks (e.g., mediation and nonconventional arbitration).

3. Police department policies that discourage interaction between police officer and citizen except for the discussion of police business or the effectuating of a police action such as arrest or issuance of summons.

4. Police administrations and a cadre of some young police officers who do not perceive mediation and nonconventional arbitration as "real police work."
(This is an even greater obstacle when administrators condone rank & file aversion of this sort, i.e., when administrators seldom reward use of nonconventional approaches to interpersonal disputes).

5. The notion held by traditionalist and inertia-bound police administrators that practices in use should not be tampered with.

6. A perception by police administrators that by way of community policing training the department is already offering interpersonal conflict/dispute resolution training when in reality it is not.

The good news is, notwithstanding the existence of the named obstacles (some of which are structural, hence very powerful), a police department can still, to some limited degree, adopt widespread use of mediation, nonconventional arbitration and other nonconventional conflict/dispute resolution methods into its operations (e.g., into scene protocol). The sections that follow demonstrate how.

MEDIATION & NONCONVENTIONAL ARBITRATION AS A WAY TO COMPLEMENT COMMUNITY POLICING INITIATIVES

There are many definitions of community policing. Perhaps, most common is the notion that community policing is a method to bring about positive relationships between police officers and the members of the communities which they serve. The use of nonconventional conflict/dispute resolution (NCDR) skills by police officers has this same goal. If patrol police officers address interpersonal disputes using mediation, nonconventional arbitration, and other nonconventional conflict/dispute resolution methods, many of the goals of community policing are realized. For example, one common goal that community policing champions is citizen empowerment. When a patrol officer offers citizens the process of mediation, he/she is conveying to them that they [citizens] are empowered to handle many of their own interpersonal disputes.

In addition, the officer who offers mediation is showing appropriate deference to the self-responsibility and freedom that many citizens expect to exercise in their lives. Both deference and empowerment, when provided by police through mediation in particular, casts a positive light on the agencies to which the officers belong. Moreover, when officers are third party intervenors, they appear less as outsiders and more as a part of the community that they serve.

Finally, it is the conflict/dispute resolution skills held by patrol police that reduce the likelihood of violent and verbal confrontation with citizens. When officers use mediation and nonconventional arbitration, they are less likely to escalate interpersonal dispute scenes with their verbal and symbolic communication. History is full of examples of social interaction between police and citizens that turned tragic. Moreover, community perception that patrol police officers have poor social interaction skills can lead to widespread dissension between police and citizens in a community.

Use of nonconventional dispute resolution skills by patrol officers should be seen as a requisite component of community policing initiatives, since both seek to foster positive police-community relations, empower citizens, show deference to citizens, and reduce confrontations between police officers and citizens.

Making NCDR Approaches A Reality: Steps to Take

In order for nonconventional conflict/dispute resolution methodologies (e.g., mediation and nonconventional arbitration) to make a positive difference in a police agency, it is necessary that their use be mandated through official proclamation. A police department must mandate that patrol officers use NCDR on scenes that warrant such methodologies. "General Orders" (or police policy handbooks) should outline when and how NCDR methods would be employed. Furthermore, there needs to be a place on a police assignment sheet (run sheet) to document use of mediation and other nonconventional methodologies (see Illustration below).

ADVICE

Run sheets should include a disposition called mediation and nonconventional arbitration. By recording these dispositions onto run sheets, data can be collected.

RUN SHEET

Scout 699   April 1, 1999

Time Dispatched	Time on Scene	Back-in-Service	Address	Nature	Disposition
0126	0129	0214	30 W. 5th Street, Apt. J	Two males arguing	Mediation
0219	0223	0251	74 W. 19th Street, Apt. 6	Man with a gun	Robbery Report Report #99888
0311	0313	0601	rear of 67 12th Street	Gun shots/ uncounscious person	Homicide Report #99889

Perhaps, in the first few years of mediation protocol, officers should be issued scene cards (see next page). Such cards will encourage use of NCDR methodologies as well as enable data collection for evaluation purposes.

SCENE CARD
For interpersonal Disputes

Check all that apply

☐ Mediation used

  ☐ Manifest issues mediated

  ☐ Underlying issues mediated

  ☐ Truce brought about via mediation

  ☐ Mediation skills used

☐ Nonconventional arbitration used

☐ Dispute was Episodic

☐ Shuttle Resolution Used

Referral to a Dispute Resolution Center ☐

Referral to other Agency ☐

Conventional Method used ☐

Scene was not amenable to mediation or nonconventional arbitration ☐

Arbitration used, but mediation was tried first ☐

Remarks and other information are written on the reverse of this card

---

In those cases in which police refer parties to a dispute resolution center, the officers should provide disputants with index cards which describe the services provided by the center as well as the center's location. A carbon copy of the card should be provided to a police department employee who will follow-up on all referrals (see Illustration on next page).[14]

REFERRAL CARD

    This card is a referral by the _____ Police Department to the City Dispute Resolution Center. Your dispute will be referred by the police department to the City Dispute Center within 24 hours. You should make an effort to contact the Center at the telephone listed below in order to have your dispute addressed. This is a free and confidential service. Your contacting the Center is voluntary; although, if you do not contact the Center within 48 hours, a representative from the police department or Center may contact you in an effort to assist you with your dispute. Your participation in this service does not result in a police report or record of the event.

                    City Dispute Resolution Center
                    1000 Main Street
                    Metropolis, State 60000
                    Tel: (777) 777-7777

    Referring Officer_____ Badge_____

    Date of Referral_____

Deference for Patrol Officers

    For a police department to fully incorporate NCDR methodologies, it will ultimately be necessary for the management style of rank and file officers to change in such a way that the patrol officer is no longer looked upon by management as simply a soldier who should not question or suggest. The role of patrol officers must be re-defined. Patrol officers must be allowed and expected to function as professionals. Furthermore, they must be given credit for knowing, better than their administrators in many cases, what is best for their beat. When supervisors consider patrol officers as key players, successful NCDR protocol implementation is possible.

Allotting Sufficient Time to NCDR Methodologies

    Police department supervisors and policies must allow for patrol officers to spend additional time on scenes where an NCDR method such as mediation is used. Many times, NCDR processes take more time than traditional responses. This is because NCDR responses represent a more substantive handling of police scenes, verses superficially handling them. A benefit of handling a scene in this way can be the reduction in repeat calls-for-service. (Mediation protocol in the Hillsboro, Oregon Police Department has reduced repeat calls-for-service.)

    Many current police systems are antagonistic to any form of scene approach that does not push for the rapid expedition of radio-runs; hence superficial handling of scenes is a trademark of many police agencies. Police agencies should realize the benefits of substantively addressing calls-for-service and understand that NCDR methodologies are an effective way to do so.

Of course, there will be times when a unit is needed back in service ASAP. These are times when informal mediation (see Chapter 1) or simply an officer's conflict/dispute resolution skills are satisfactory alternatives (on a scene).

Additional Criteria for Rewards

Police departments routinely reward patrol officers for heroism when the officer shoots a suspect. However, seldom are officers rewarded who defuse and calm situations (e.g., potential riots) through the use of good conflict/dispute resolution skills.

By adopting NCDR methodologies, a department must be prepared to reward and meritoriously decorate officers who employ mediation and other NCDR methods and as a result avert serious situations.

Stay Cognizant of Professionalism & Science

The application of mediation and nonconventional arbitration implies two elements:

1. Professional application;
2. Scientific application (or systematic application).

On one level, professional application is defined as the officer possessing the requisite education and training to enable his/her employment of methods such as mediation. On another level, professional application signifies polite, lawful, and objective delivery of the mediation process among others. Systematic (scientific) application emphasizes the step-by-step by process in which the officer demonstrates analytical ability and learned skills. Adherence to the scientific method enables patrol police officers to handle their tasks substantively rather than superficially.

The officer who satisfies the criteria presented for professional application and has a commitment to systematically handling scenes will fair well in his/her practice of mediation, nonconventional arbitration, and other nonconventional conflict/dispute resolution methodologies.

Professionalization (not to be confused with the "Professional model/era" of policing which was preoccupied with administrative and procedural objectives) in policing refers to giving policing a more learned professional character. This occurs in a police agency in large part when police officers who comprise the agency are professionals as a result of their having received formal, academic education concerning the profession, as well as having special skills pertinent to the practice of the profession. Professionalization also characterizes an agency in which many organizational tasks are performed in a systematic process.

Since conceptualization, comprehension, and employment of mediation and other NCDR methodologies sometimes requires that a patrol officer have a strong academic base, it would be helpful if a police agency underwent a transformation to professionalization prior to providing its patrol police officers with training to employ nonconventional conflict/dispute resolution methodologies. However, the fact that professionalization of many police agencies typically occurs piece-meal enables us to recognize that incorporation of methodologies such as mediation and nonconventional arbitration can also occur piecemeal.

Granted, college educated police officers are more likely than non-college educated officers to fully comprehend NCDR training and methodologies. However, officers with less external education can also fair well with proper, perhaps protracted training. At a minimum, all officers should receive basic, formal training in nonconventional arbitration, mediation, and other nonconventional conflict/dispute resolution methodologies. Dispute resolution organizations can provide trainers to police departments for this purpose. Second, a substantial (verses not complete) commitment by a police department to systematic and substantive handling of calls-for-service is necessary for NCDR methodologies to become effective tools within a police department.

CHAPTER 4
CURRICULUM MODELS & BILLETS FOR PATROL OFFICERS

Uniformed police officers assigned to patrol duties (e.g., foot patrol, scout or unit car, and scooter) benefit from having nonconventional conflict/dispute resolution training. They are the street cops who often represent the first government response, literally and physically, to an interpersonal conflict/dispute. The patrol officer's role in the interpersonal conflict resolution arena occurs frequently. So, it's appropriate that training that improves on the handling of interpersonal disputes is delivered to patrol police officers.

By teaching patrol police officers nonconventional conflict/dispute resolution skills, you are enabling them to:

• Show professionalism on the part of themselves and their department;
• Contribute to a decrease in citizen complaints against the police;
• Contribute to a reduction in repeat calls-for-service, hence scout cars and beat officers are in-service[15] longer or responding to pressing emergencies;
• Contribute to improved police-citizen relations;
• Contribute to a decrease in the need by patrol officers to use physical force;
• Manage scenes professionally and systematically.

Following are three models of NCDR training for patrol police officers.[16]

The first model, *General/Familiarity Conflict Resolution Training* (or general interpersonal conflict resolution training) instructs patrol police officers on the importance of conflict/dispute resolution skills in patrol police work. This general training familiarizes police officers with mediation, nonconventional arbitration, and other methodologies. Typically, this is short-term instruction (e.g., two three-hour sessions), although it could be longer term. This training is not intended to have an influence on police policy or to make officers proficient in the use of any particular NCDR method. However, for some officers who undergo the training, it will be tremendously helpful to their social interaction with citizens.

The second model is called *Triage Training*. Officers are taught how to identify and refer the types of interpersonal disputes which are appropriate, or legislatively mandated for referral to conflict/dispute resolution centers. The idea is to prepare police officers to become triage agents.[17] Although not an active interventionist approach, discerning which cases are appropriate for a referral to a conflict/dispute resolution center is an important police charge. Triage training is crucial since it is intended to instill mandated protocol and behaviors. This training should be at least fifteen hours, if possible.

The third curriculum model is called *Full Responsibility Training*. This training is the most substantive of the three types. Police officers are given instruction which, at the conclusion of training, will certify them to practice one or more nonconventional conflict/dispute resolution methodologies. An example of full responsibility training is substantive mediation training which prepares officers to become full-fledged mediators. In short, the idea of full responsibility training is to enable officers to handle scenes without making a referral.

Note that even though by full responsibility training the officer is certified as a conflict resolution professional (or mediator, for example), he/she is still expected to make referrals to a conflict/dispute resolution center for matters which require more extensive and formal attention (than even a police officer who is a conflict/dispute resolution professional can offer). In this way, the officer is a triage agent when necessary and the trained professional/practitioner when necessary. It is sort of a hybrid role that officers are able to undertake. That role is called the *Full Responsibility-Triage Hybrid*. Consider, that if officers only have triage training, they are often acting as peripheral agents to an interpersonal dispute. In fact, there is a risk that the scene may not be substantively handled because of the passive role of the responding police. A hybrid model of Full Responsibility-Triage enables the officer to be an integral player in the resolution of the dispute, notwithstanding that the officer may refer the dispute.

Full responsibility training prepares police officers to assume full responsibility for employment of nonconventional conflict/dispute resolution methodologies. The training provided to police officers that enables them to take full responsibly for a scene teaches them to scientifically (or systematically or methodologically) employ a methodology or methodologies. It is suggested that this training occur in twenty-five to fifty hours and include additional periodic refresher training as necessary.[18]

NOTE

Full Responsibility training provides instruction/training to police officers that enables them to become competent conflict/dispute resolution professionals.

When a department elects to have its officers given full responsibility training, it should also provide officers with the discretion to decide whether to mediate and, more importantly, that the officer is allowed the additional time which may be needed to do so. Many police departments do not allow officers the necessary time to handle many calls-for-service in a substantive manner. Often, the standard practice is to handle as many calls as possible and as rapidly as possible. Too much time spent on a run, although legitimate, is often perceived as "milking a run." In a nut shell, for many police departments, accepting the *Full*

Responsibility model will entail extensive altering of policy and scene protocol.

At the conclusion of some form of NCDR training, the officer is either a generalist, a triage agent, or a full responsibility agent.

NCDR TRAINING TYPES FOR PATROL OFFICERS

NCDR Training Types for Patrol Police Officers

1. General/Familiarity Conflict Resolution Training
2. Triage Training
3. Full Responsibility Training

Cooper, 1998
COPYRIGHT ©

CHAPTER 5
THE ROLE OF EXTERNAL
CONFLICT/DISPUTE RESOLUTION TRAINERS

This chapter provides information and a how-to guide for the dispute resolution professional who administers or wants to administer interpersonal conflict/dispute resolution training (specifically mediation and nonconventional arbitration) to patrol police officers.

In your role as a trainer of patrol police, the crux of your mission is "To train patrol police officers to better manage police scenes at which there is an interpersonal dispute." Mediation and nonconventional arbitration are the most important nonconventional methodologies that you can teach patrol police officers. (Additionally, nonconventional methods include problem solving and facilitation [after all, we want police officers to convene community meetings now and then, etc.]) These methods can be pragmatically and effectively applied by police officers in accomplishing patrol objectives.

Many dispute resolution professionals have an interest in providing interpersonal conflict/dispute training to/for police officers. However, there is reluctance by many police agencies, for a variety of reasons, to contract with dispute resolution professionals for this purpose. One reason in particular for the resistance is a lack of awareness by many police administrators that the training exists. Many administrators have heard of mediation, but may not have heard about mediation for use by street cops. It is important to provide police administrators with information on the benefits of using mediation and other NCDR skills in patrol police work.

Other police administrators incorrectly assume that they are already offering substantive mediation and nonconventional arbitration training when they are not. Often what is being offered is training to promote the practice of community policing. Although, the training includes a component related to handling interpersonal disputes, a closer examination of the training shows that it lacks:
- Certified conflict resolution trainers;
- Specific focus on relevant methodologies and awareness of distinctions between the methodologies;
- Adequate academic depth;
- Applications of the methodologies in a scientific (systematic) manner.

Obtaining Contracts: The Police Department as Solicitor

In some cases, police administrators request the training services of conflict/dispute resolution professionals. The hope is that the training will bolster existing community-policing initiatives. In fact, the creation of contracts for this purpose is laudable, since the community policing-minded administrator is likely to make the connection between nonconventional conflict/dispute resolution skills and community policing.

Other reasons that explain why police administrators look to conflict/dispute resolution professionals and trainers for assistance include:

1. To find the best way to respond to an interpersonal crisis (e.g., widespread citizen-police dissension);
2. To explore ways to improve relations between police and citizens;
3. To find ways to decrease excessive police force incidents;
4. To learn about conflict resolution methods that can decrease repeat calls-for-service;
5. To bolster the department's image.

When the police department is the solicitor, the trainer is likely to have an advantage, since he/she will not have to invest time to overcome administrative resistance (or lack of awareness) to mediation, nonconventional arbitration, and other NCDR training. However, there are times when a department may have solicited the training, but that same department is not enthusiastic about receiving the training. This is likely the case when the police department's reason for requesting the training is not based on a genuine desire to partake in the instruction. For example, if a request for training was in response to public pressure on the police department to bring about police reform because of the manner by which the police handled a situation (e.g., allegation of unnecessary, excessive force). The incident may have escalated as a result of an improper conflict/dispute resolution method employed by the police. In response, members of the community, perhaps with the assistance of local politicians, demanded not only an investigation into the incident, but also shifts in policy and procedures to incorporate better or additional training of the municipality's police officers.

Even if a police department has contracted for training for the wrong reasons, the trainer may still be able to deliver effective training. With an appropriate training stratagem, a trainer may be able to overcome tremendous obstacles.

The Trainer as Solicitor

The salesperson savvy that may often prove successful in the corporate world will not fair well in selling many police departments on the idea of contracting for conflict/dispute resolution training. The nuances and peculiarities of police work, especially regarding police solidarity, mean that a salesperson needs more than brilliant salespersonship. Selling conflict/dispute resolution training to a police department requires knowing a great deal about police work, police solidarity, police history (literature), common police notions, and official police protocol (operating and scene procedures).

When the police department has not approached the trainer, the trainer may have a formidable task in trying to convince police administrators that the training is worthwhile, beneficial, and necessary. Care must be taken when calling attention to a problem that could alienate the prospective client. If the trainer recognizes factors which show the need for conflict/dispute resolution training (e.g., strife between members of visible minority groups and the police), he/she will have to make a judgment call as to which, if any, of these factors will appear in the training proposal.

When attempting to receive a contract for training services, write a letter of introduction, accompanied by a short proposal. In writing the proposal, take into account the orientation of the police department you are soliciting. It is important to write a proposal that appeals to the department to which you seek to deliver training. (See next section for more information about department orientation.)

The letter or initial contact should include descriptions by the trainer as to how conflict/dispute resolution training (e.g., mediation and/or nonconventional arbitration) can benefit the department, its officers, and the communities which the department serves. Feel free to list the benefits as I have listed them in this book (please use citations when necessary though). Additionally, you (the trainer) should indicate why you are the appropriate person (or the entity that you represent) to deliver the training.

Attempt to obtain letters of support from other law enforcement agencies that have undergone some form of interpersonal conflict/dispute resolution training. Make sure to include these letters in the packet that you send to your prospective client. Another idea which proved successful for a trainer (according to his testimony at the 1997 Conference of the Society of Professionals in Dispute Resolution), is to approach a police agency and offer to write a grant for the department in order to acquire the financial resources to enter into a contract with the agency. The grant would fund a dispute resolution initiative such as mediation referral arrangements or mediation training for police officers. Finally, in some cases, trainers should offer mediation and nonconventional arbitration training, etc., to police agencies pro bono. This makes sense as a way to get a foot in the door as a police trainer.

Department Orientation as a Determinant of Type & Intensity of Training & Malleability Issues

Police organization philosophy
influences how patrol services are delivered

The character of a police department and the primary duties of a police department will greatly determine the manner, type, and intensity of conflict/dispute resolution training that the conflict/dispute resolution professional will deliver.

In a general sense, knowing the character and orientation of a police department which is a prospective or definite client enables a trainer to gauge the department's amenability to nonconventional conflict/dispute resolution training. On another level, knowing the orientation of the targeted police department enables the trainer to gauge malleability issues such as determining how much influence the training will have, if any, on police policy (essentially, whether the training will lead to policy changes such as in scene protocol).

Given that police departments, like most other things, come in a variety of forms and shapes, let us examine several types of police department orientations (there are many others which are not addressed here).

A department with a heavily legalistic or heavily militaristic orientation (e.g., some state police agencies) is likely characterized by strict enforcement of laws. Officers employ little discretion and hence are seldom flexible. Moreover, social interaction between officer and citizen is usually characterized by an indifferent, stern, and rigid demeanor on the part of the officer. Social interaction with citizens for purposes other than for law enforcement reasons is less common and not necessarily sought by the officers. This type of agency, perhaps, would be least receptive to having its officers undergo NCDR training. Nevertheless, conflict/dispute resolution trainers must identify ways to appeal to agencies of this sort. Perhaps, militaristic or legalistic departments may be more willing to accept the services of a trainer for the purpose of officers receiving "general familiarity" conflict resolution training rather than training which would re-orient the department.

Municipal police agencies (e.g., city and town police departments), public school law enforcement agencies, and even hospital and university police departments tend to be agencies more open to interpersonal conflict resolution training. Often, these agencies have established policing initiatives that utilize communities as resources (i.e., police departments adhering to a community policing philosophy or having community policing programs). Nonconventional conflict/dispute resolution training can be seen as a complement to either the philosophy of the department or, in the case of a program, the tenets of the program.

NOTE

A trainer must note that sometimes a police department has more than one orientation.

It is prudent for a trainer preparing to approach a police department (or in preparing for a training), to try to determine early-on how much change the police department is willing to undertake and to plan the training accordingly. Furthermore, knowing the orientation of the police department enables the trainer to gauge the level of department interest and enthusiasm that there would be for training.

Methods for Delivering Training[19]

Training should include the following five steps:

Step 1: The introduction by the coordinator or designated trainer in which all trainers (team members) are introduced.

Step 2: Breaking the Ice: An Interest, Trust, and Confidence Building Presentation[20].

Step 3: Opening the session to questions and answers.

Step 4: Delivery of training via lecture.

Step 5: Delivery of training via participant involvement (e.g., role-playing).

All lectures should be followed by an activity in which the officers have an active role, as when a discussion is opened for questions and answers. Although question and answer periods are important in nonconventional conflict/dispute resolution training sessions (they enable for a decrease in police officer resistance to the training), trainers should heed a word of caution: Do not allow questions from officers to precede the initial introductory presentation or to dominate the introductory presentation. Resentment of the trainers and lack of interest in the training held by many of the officers can crash right into the trainer with such force that the possibility of delivering an effective training session thereafter will cease. Any salvaging may be impossible. Step 2 (above) can dissipate a lot of resentment and lack of interest at the outset, provided that Step 2 occurs rapidly on the heels of Step 1 and is well planned. Simply stated, the trainer's actions must enable for Step 2 to occur.

METHOD OF DELIVERING CONFLICT RESOLUTION TRAINING TO PATROL OFFICERS

1. Introduction by coordinator
2. Breaking the Ice: An Interest, Trust, & Confidence Building Presentation (trainers with police experience are the best persons to deliver this step)
3. Questions and answers
4. Delivery of training: Lecture
5. Delivery of training: Participant involvement (e.g., role playing)

Cooper 1996
COPYRIGHT©

It is seldom the case that officers are extremely disrespectful of trainers. The lack of interest and resentment will likely come in a respectful and even a professional tone and manner.

Step 2 creates a stratagem to enable for effective training. Specifically, Step 2 has the following major objectives:

1. Reducing police officer skepticism of the training and trainers;
2. Demonstrating that beliefs by police officers that there is nothing that the trainer can possibly teach them are inaccurate;
3. Transforming a lack of interest by many of the police officers into enthusiastic participation in the training.

The strategy for trainers achieving a degree of acceptance necessitates having a trainer with police experience perform Step 2.[21] Through the trainer's empathy, knowledge of police protocol, shared experiences, and place in the police subculture, that individual can quickly bring about trust, confidence, and interest in the training as well as trust of, and confidence and interest in the trainers on the part of the police officers. The trainer with police officer experience, and because of his/her experience, can effectively deal with the resistance to the training and trainers. The standing of a trainer with police experience is further bolstered by his/her showing:

1. That he/she has walked in their (officers/trainees) shoes. This can be done by describing real-life scenes at which he/she was present;
2. That he/she knows from personal police experience that nonconventional conflict/dispute resolution skills are effective in achieving police ends;
3. That use of nonconventional conflict/dispute resolution skills is not a sign of weakness on the part of the police officer, and that a police officer can still be a crime-fighter and law enforcer contemporaneous with employing nonconventional conflict/dispute resolution methodologies.

SOCIAL WORKER AVERSION

Police resistance to nonconventional conflict/dispute resolution training is in some part related to the aversion by many police officers for duties perceived as social worker duties (Note that social work and social service are distinguishable from one another in police circles. It is the former which draws the bulk of criticism from some police officers.) Nonconventional conflict/dispute resolution methodologies (as duties) are perceived by some police officers as "social worker duties." Many police officers do not wish their mandate to be associated with the duties of a social worker. Any task identified in police officer circles as having the hint of a social worker's duties is quickly marked as not real police work. Many police officers fail to realize that performing police work incorporates many of the duties of social workers. Moreover, many police officers just don't realize that patrol, police officers have been performing social worker duties since the beginning of modern policing. Arming police officers with nonconventional conflict/dispute resolution skills and expecting them to employ them professionally and scientifically, is simply a way to perfect what police have been doing all along.

In the event that a trainer with police experience is on your team, have him/her describe to trainees how police officers can benefit from the conflict/dispute resolution training. This must be done through examples of real-life situations of the type that the officers have likely encountered. For example, I present to police officers real-life situations via examples of my personal experiences as a police officer. More importantly, I convey how nonconventional conflict/dispute resolution methodologies were used on a scene, or if they had not been used, how they would have enabled for success (hence, effectuated scene management). The types of situations (scenes) that I present to illustrate the importance of nonconventional conflict/dispute resolution skills follow:

1. Domestic situations not involving violence.

2. Shooting scenes (e.g., the police come upon the body of a man shot to death in a robbery) in which disputes erupt between onlookers.

3. Assist with property or a dispute over property. For example, a boyfriend and girlfriend have ended their co-habitation. One of the parties has agreed to move from the dwelling. He/she wants to remove a piece of property from the dwelling and the other party does not want to part with the property. The police have been summoned to assist in resolving the dispute.

4. Disbursing large crowds that include groups antagonistic to one another. These are, typically situations where the original disputing parties have been arrested (i.e., for physically fighting) and the police have the task of separating and disbursing other parties. These situations often explode/escalate when police mishandle them. The fact the parties may be disorderly should not warrant an attempt at mass arrest. The sheer number of people, which many times far outnumbers the police, warrants the scientific (systematic) use of nonconventional conflict/dispute resolution skills.

5. A police officer responding to a scene (one in which a crime had not been committed) that a fellow officer had previously responded to, but [the previous officer] neglected to address the dispute. The first responding officer, by his/her failure to substantively handle the scene the first time, has created a situation in which the police are once again summoned (a repeat call: the dispatcher sends another unit to the scene).

This example is particularly significant, since many officers do not like finishing other officers unfinished work. For this reason, many officers will be pleased to hear the trainer announce that nonconventional conflict/dispute resolution skills can lead to a decrease in repeat responses to a scene as well as a reduction in lazy co-workers.

Once again, note that there are increased benefits when offering scene typologies along with examples of situations where the trainer was present as a police officer. One such benefit is in the form of a message of empathy and shared experiences.

HINT
Training teams of two that consist of one with police experience make for progress.

> **NOTE**
> It is beneficial for a conflict/dispute resolution trainer of police officers to have police experience. This experience can represent an icebreaker in training sessions. The experience enables for the trainer to empathize if necessary. Even more important, the trainer who was once (or still is) a police officer can overcome resistance to the training and skepticism of the trainers.

Many trainers are not current or former police officers. Certainly, it would be to a trainer's benefit to team-up with conflict/dispute resolution professionals who have police experience or to team-up with police officers who have undergone conflict/dispute resolution training and are willing to offer positive testimony at training sessions about nonconventional conflict/dispute resolution skills.

That is not to say that a trainer without police experience is destined to fail. On the contrary, provided that trainers without police experience become familiar faces in police circles as well as build positive relationships within those circles. Then, even in situations when the trainer is addressing a new group, the trainer's extensive knowledge of police scene protocol and the police sub-culture proves extremely effective in gaining officer trust and confidence.[22]

The use of skits or role-plays in which police officers participate represent a highly successful training method. Role-plays should mirror the types of scenes which the officers will encounter. Designing realistic role-plays necessitates knowledge of common police behavior at a variety of police scenes. For example, the trainer must be familiar with official police protocol (for the "specific" department) that may be required alongside the use of nonconventional conflict/dispute resolution methodologies (e.g., notification of a police official concerning a certain activity, having to remain on a scene until an official arrives, or report filing and other activities mandated by police department policy).[23] (See Chapter 1, role plays are provided.) Additionally, role plays must incorporate "officer safety" protocol.

> **NOTE**
> Make sure to tailor your training to each group of officers and to the duties that they perform.

NINE KEY POINTS TO REMEMBER IF YOU ARE A CONFLICT/DISPUTE RESOLUTION PROFESSIONAL WHO TRAINS POLICE OFFICERS

1. When soliciting a police department/agency, it is beneficial that you (the trainer) know the orientation(s) of the agency (community policing is an example of an orientation). If approached by a law enforcement agency, you should inquire as to the orientation of the agency.

2. You must firmly establish what type of training the department expects you to offer. The many distinguishable duties of law enforcement officers necessitate job-specific conflict/dispute resolution training in many cases.

3. In determining the type and depth of training which you will offer, determine how much change the police organization is prepared to undertake in incorporating nonconventional conflict/dispute resolution methodologies. Hence, make sure to

4. Recognize that you will likely encounter some resistance from administrators in your quest to convince a police department to accept nonconventional conflict/dispute resolution training.

5. Recognize that at the start of any training (and throughout the training if particular phenomena are not addressed), you will likely encounter moderate to extreme resistance from rank-and-file police officers. Recognize that the resistance will be, in large part, the result of a belief nonconventional conflict/dispute resolution methods will not work in the communities in which they patrol.

6. It is beneficial for a conflict/dispute resolution trainer of police officers to have police experience. His/her empathy and shared experiences with trainees overcomes resistance to training.

7. At the start of a training, you must be prepared to deal with and contradict two common police notions:
   - That common sense is all that a police officer needs to be an effective police officer;
   - That a police officer does not have time to be analytical (the latter includes the incorrect notion that being analytical will get a cop killed).

8. Police solidarity is unlike solidarity bonds in other professions. A trainer must always be cognizant of this fact. Usually, police solidarity is reserved for police officers (includes former and retired). The trainer will need access in order to deliver effective training. A trainer must not be personally offended by this phenomenon. He/she must have a plan or strategy which will enable the amount of acceptance necessary to deliver effective training. The plan or strategy must be genuine, incorporate empathy if possible, and include the delivery of training that relates police work to nonconventional conflict/dispute resolution skills.

9. Effective training has been delivered by the trainer when the majority of police officers participating have adequately accepted the training, and when the principles, skills, and knowledge conveyed by the trainer are accurate and as complete as warranted by contract expectation and agreement (including satisfaction of training objectives).

CURRICULUM FOR A FULL RESPONSIBILITY-TRIAGE HYBRID TRAINING

(1) Explain the distinction between a conflict and a dispute (e.g., Latent v. Manifest)

(2) Explain the distinction between interpersonal and intrapersonal.

(3) Explain what is meant by the term third party intervenor (let the officer know that he/she is receiving skills which will enhance his/her role as a third party intervenor in interpersonal disputes).

(4) With participation from the officers, identify conventional methods of handling interpersonal dispute scenes.

(5) Identify nonconventional methods. Make sure to explain what was is meant by NCDR (Noncoventional Conflict/Dispute Resolution).

(6) Explain symbolic interactionism. It is especially important that officers learn how their facial expressions and body language can escalate a scene or calm a scene.

(7) Cultural differences for which the officer must be cognizant. (Read Thorston Sellin's (1968) research, see the bibliography)

(8) Ask officers to name ground rules that a person would expect the other to follow if he were involved in an interpersonal dispute with the other.

(9) Conflict/Dispute Resolution Skills
I v. You statements
Statements never to make: e.g., "It never happens" "You are always..., etc."
Never make statements that back people into a corner: e.g., "Your mother... etc."
Statements about a person's race or sexuality
Conduct listening exercises

(10) Deliver Professional Arbitration instruction.

(11) Conduct Professional Arbitration exercises and role plays.

(12) Deliver Mediation instruction.
Don't forget to talk about power imbalances.
Don't forget to talk about conducting mediation unbeknownst to the disputants.
Don't forget to talk about how mediation skills can reduce the likelihood of an officer receiving a reprimand.

(13) Conduct Mediation exercises and role plays.

(14) Deliver Facilitation instruction. Officers need to know how to facilitate communication, between groups especially.

(15) Conduct Facilitation exercises and role plays.

(16) Deliver Problem Solving instruction. (I suggest that you read Herman Goldstein's Problem Oriented Policing (1990) before conducting the training.)

(17) Conduct Problem Solving exercises and role plays.

CHAPTER 6
TWO POLICE DEPARTMENT MEDIATION PROGRAMS

THE HILLSBORO POLICE DEPARTMENT MEDIATION PROGRAM

"One of the interesting things that I had happen when we
started doing mediations is people kept coming up and saying…
you simply can't mediate a a police officer…that's not true"
— *Officer Ed Vance, 18 year veteran, HPD*

In 1996, with the help of a grant from the Oregon Dispute Resolution Commission, the Hillsboro Police Department (HPD) developed and established a program called the Hillsboro mediation program. The impetus of the program, described as a "Community Policing Journey" by its creator Patti Williams, was to reduce repeat calls-for-service regarding neighborhood disputes. In due time, the focus remained on repeat calls, but the mediation program took-on addressing a variety of interpersonal conflicts. (In some cases, patrol officers offer people a choice between receiving a citation or scheduling a mediation.)

In the furtherance of enhancing the Mediation Program, the HPD had the program coordinator administer a 32-hour mediation skills training to several officers (as well as other police department personnel). The coordinator pointed out that the training had a goal of helping the officers to be cognizant of the "bigger picture" when dealing with criminal (or problematic) behaviors they are typically called to handle. "To look beyond the specific behavior [of the disputants] to discover the initial cause of the behavior."

To let the community know that officers would soon be about putting their new skills to use, the HPD had program members address local civic groups among a variety of other groups. Citizens were told about the mediation services offered by the HPD and the benefits of using mediation to resolve interpersonal disputes. Today, patrol personnel carry brochures which describe the program. The brochures are also used as the referral form which is provided to disputants. As to the latter, the program coordinator is notified of all such patrol contacts, and if one of the involved parties does not call the program within 48 hours, the coordinator contacts them (e.g., to set up a mediation).

The Hillsboro Police Department recently began providing the 32-hour Mediation Skill Training (equivalent to a full responsibility training, see Chapter 4) to all of its police officers. The goal is continue to increase referrals, but as well to enable officers to conduct formal mediation on a scene if necessary and if time permits. The training represents the triage-full responsibility hybrid role that officers can undertake in delivering nonconventional dispute resolution services such as mediation. Recall, the hybrid represents that the officer has undergone training which credentials him/her as a dispute resolution professional capable of conducting mediation, but as well (the hybrid aspect), the officer sometimes functions as a triage agent.

In the ten months that this service has been available, there have been no repeat calls-for-service to citizens who have received mediation services. The program has been such a success that it has been made a permanent line item in the city's budget. Clearly, the Hillsboro program is above reproach. Its cutting-edge, exemplary model is worthy of replication in other jurisdictions.

For more information, contact Program Coordinator Patti Williams, or Chief of Police, Ron Louie, or Mediator/Officer Ed Vance at the Hillsboro Police Department: Tel: (503) 681-6491 Fax: (503) 681-6107 E-mail: pattiw@cl.hillsboro.or.us

THE PITTSBURGH POLICE BUREAU
*"The Police Officer who chooses to use conflict resolution
and mediation skills, will take policing to another level. On this level,
the officer will have community respect, trust, and admiration."*
— *Jerome Jackson, Pittsburgh Mediation Center Trainer*

In October 1997, the Pittsburgh Police Bureau Pittsburgh Police Department) officially mandated mediation protocol for responses to calls-for-service (see the Order on the next page). The protocol calls for officers to be trained according to a triage model as described in Chapter 4. Recall, that the model represents that patrol officers are trained to identify interpersonal disputes amenable to mediation, then to refer such cases to dispute resolution centers where disputants can have their case mediated, among a variety of other alternatives. The order includes a requirement that all Pittsburgh Police Bureau officers must undergo general conflict resolution training, e.g., The training emphasizes active-listening, cultural and racial diversity phenomena, and communication skills.

The Pittsburgh Police Bureau and the Pittsburgh Mediation Center (PMC) jointly coordinate the Pittsburgh Police Bureau Mediation Referred Project. The PMC takes referrals from Pittsburgh patrol police officers. In the near future, the PMC will begin a program for police academy instructors called "Train the Trainers." Upon completion of the program, the police instructors will be qualified to teach a six-hour conflict resolution class to police cadets as well as other officers.

NOTE

Commenting on conflict resolution training for police officers in Pittsburgh, Commander Regina McDonald of the Pittsburgh Police Bureau [Department] states that a training team must "bring in police officers for input; scenarios must demonstrate proper officer safety skills; and the training has to be adapted to the needs of the police officers."

The Pittsburgh Police Bureau protocol and the PMC Mediation Referral Project are worth replicating.

For more information, contact Commander Regina McDonald at the Pittsburgh Police Bureau or one of the following at the Pittsburgh Mediation Center: Gale McGloin, Executive Director or one of the following, Jerome Jackson, Shelly Cottom, or Ellen DeBenedetti. Tel: (412)381 4443 Fax: (412)381 5334 E-mail:pmc@trfn.cipgh.org

Chiefs order in part.
Reprinted with permission of Pittsburgh Police Bureau,

CITY OF PITTSBURGH BUREAU OF POLICE
Office of the Chief
(accountability, integrity, respect)
October 30, 1997

Conflict Resolution and Mediation– Policy/Purpose To provide all members of the Bureau of Police with a protocol to follow for those incidents and or disputes where mediation may be a reasonable alternative to a more conventional law enforcement intervention method.

Types of Cases Eligible for Conflict/Resolution Mediation

Neighborhood Disputes, including but not limited to the following: Parking disputes, property line disputes, animal control complaints, neighborhood children, noise/loud music complaints, Landlord/Tenant Disputes, Family Disputes (outside of "normal" domestic violent incidents).

Community policing officers have been trained in ...conflict resolution and will be initially referred to those cases where conflict resolution/mediation is a reasonable alternative. A member of the Bureau of Police (e.g., an officer) who identifies a situation that may benefit from conflict resolution/mediation should first file an offense/incident report detailing the following information:

1. The nature of the dispute
2. Pertinent information of all involved parties (names, addresses, phone numbers) etc. ...

END NOTES

1. Conflict/dispute resolution training can teach police officers how to best deal with intrapersonal conflict or how they can best contend with the stresses of police work; however, this book does not concern such phenomena. Rather, chiefly in issue is the training given to police officers to enable them to better manage police scenes in which there is an interpersonal conflict or dispute.

2. For those unfamiliar with police terminology, in-service mean that the unit (e.g., a police car) is available for dispatch to an assignment.

3. Cf. Bittner, 1990

4. The term formal relates to adherence to the mediation process and has nothing to do with the venue in which the mediation occurs. Moreover, the fact that the mediation occurs in a venue other than an office does not make the process informal. This author believes that here is a commonly held notion in the dispute resolution discipline (e.g., see Slaikeu, 1989) that the determination of whether a mediation is formal or informal is gauged by the venue in which the mediation occurs. On the contrary, I posit that determining formal verses informal, depends on whether or not there is full or staggered/partial adherence, by the mediator, to the procedural steps of the mediation process. Full adherence represents formal mediation, where as, staggered or partial adherence represents informal mediation.

5. It is not recommended to place a limit on the number of disputants. For example, there can be ten disputants.

6. Many disputes in which there have been contemporaneous physical violence between disputants are not appropriate for patrol police officer mediation [on the scene]. In some jurisdictions, these types of disputes are sometimes addressed by post-adjudication mediation.

7. This concept (CMM) has been created by the author (Cooper).

8. Issues of equity law are also pertinent.

9. This author is not going to assert that every assist with property call involves parties who want to forget the past and go on with their lives. On the contrary, there are times when an assist with property call is either a guise to encourage a confrontation of underlying issues or that underlying issues cloud the possibility of realistic property demands. Relative to this author's proposal, there will be assist with property scenes at which the patrol officer will need to shift from mediation or another conflict resolution method, preferably another "nonconventional" method (e.g., arbitration).

10 Try not to use the word control. This word may suggest to a disputant that you are taking away his/her free will.

11. It is common for notes taken by mediator and disputants in a mediation, to be destroyed following the mediation - a practice in line with confidential safeguards of the mediation process. Consider that officers' field notes are seldom destroyed. Perhaps then, it must be accepted that some notes will remain in existence fol-

lowing a mediation.

12. The pitfalls must be watched for throughout the mediation process, but especially during brainstorming for possible resolutions.

13. If you said "stop" then you got the point if you said "go" you are right.

14. In Orland Park, Illinois the Orland Park Police Department's official adoption of mediation protocol includes a memorandum generated for any location to which the police have reported at least three times in a one year period. The memorandum is provided to an officer who has the responsibility of evaluating the situation for possible mediation.

15. For those unfamiliar with police terminology. in-service means that the unit is available to be dispatched to an assignment.

16. Titles and definitions of the three approaches are those of the author.

17. Cf. Volpe, 1980. She addresses two major uses of mediation by police: mediation as an intervention strategy by police officers and the role of police officers in referring cases to conflict/dispute resolution centers.

18. Unfortunately, it is not common for police officers to receive such extensive training. Nor do many police administrators expect their officers to possess this level of competence.

19. The term trainee can be used to convey points. It is not recommended that in training sessions trainers refer to police officers as trainees. Other terms are more appropriate.

20. The name which identifies this step is that of the author of this book. The step is based on a format created by Carole Eldridge (1996) of the Dispute Resolution Center for Ottawa-Carleton. The format proved a success in training sessions.

21. As a member of Carole Eldridge's team (see previous endnote), in delivering training, the author of this book delivers the step two presentation.

22. Step two presentations can be effected in part by trainers not having police experience, by their showing police officers the relevancy of the training to police duties.

23. I suggest that trainers of police officers who do not have police experience, arrange to partake in what are called ride-alongs. These are situations in which civilians accompany police officers on patrol as observers. Ride-alongs will bolster a trainer's knowledge of police protocol and the police sub-culture.

BIBLIOGRAPHY

Baker, (1986). *Cops:Their lives in their own words*. New York: Simon and Schuster.

Bard, M. (1975). *The function of the police in crisis intervention and conflict management*. Washington, D.C.: U.S. Department of Justice.

Bard, M. (1973). *Family crisis intervention: From concept to implementation*. Washington, D.C.: U.S. Department of Justice.

Bard, M. (1970). *Training police as specialists in family crisis intervention*. Washington, D.C.: U.S. Department of Justice.

Bittner, E. (1990). *Aspects of police work*. Boston: Northeastern University Press.

Black, D. (1980). *The manners and customs of the police*. New York: Academic Press.

Cooper, C. (1997). *"Patrol Police Officer Conflict Resolution Processes." Journal of Criminal Justice*, 25, 2, 87-101.

Cooper, C. (1996). *Conflict: Conflict/Dispute Resolution Training & Police Officers*. Copenhagen, Denmark: University of Copenhagen, Sociologisk Institut.

Fisher, R., Ury, W., & Patton (1981). *Getting to yes: Negotiating agreement without giving in (2nd ed)*. New York: Penguin Books.

Folberg, J. and Taylor, A. (1984). *Mediation: A comprehensive guide to resolving conflict without litigation*. San Francisco: Jossey-Bass.

Goldstein, H. (1990). *Problem oriented policing*. New York: McGraw-Hill.

Lawson, P. (1982). *Somebody else's blues: A study of police mediation activities*. Washington, D.C.: University Press of America.

Meeks, D. (1993). "Dispute Resolution and law resolution and law enforcement in the 1990s: A system design." *Journal of California Law Enforcement, 27,* 3:98-99.

Muir, W. (1977). *Police: Streetcorner politicians*. Chicago: University of Chicago Press.

Slaikeu, K. (1996). *When push comes to shove: A practical guide to mediating disputes*. San Francisco: Jossey-Bass.

Sellin, T. (1938). "The conflict of conduct norms." *The Social Science Research Council Bulletin 41*, 63-70.

Volpe, M. and Christian, T. (1989, June 15). "Mediation: New addition to cop's toolbox." *Law Enforcement News*, 8-13.

Volpe, M. (1989). The police role. In M. Wright and B. Ã Galaway, *Mediation and criminal justice: Victims, offenders, and community*. Newbury Park: SAGE.

Williams, P. (1997, Fall). Police and mediation: A win-win partnership. *The Oregon Police Chief*, 25-26.

NAME AND SUBJECT INDEX

ABOUT THE AUTHOR

Christopher Cooper, J.D., Ph.D. is an Assistant Professor of Sociology/ Criminal Justice with a specialization in Policing and Conflict/Dispute Resolution, at Saint Xavier University. He is a Post Doctorate Fulbright Scholar & Lecturer (Denmark, 1996). Fulbright research was an analysis of the study of police officer conflict resolution methodologies. Dr. Cooper is a former United States Marine, Metropolitan [Washington, D.C.] Police Officer, and is Chair of the Society of Professionals in Dispute Resolution (SPIDR) Criminal Justice Sector. He has conducted conflict/dispute resolution training in the United States, England, Canada, Ukraine, and Denmark among many other venues. Dr. Cooper's other publications include:

Cooper, C. (1997). Patrol Police Officer Conflict Resolution Processes. *Journal of Criminal Justice*, 25, 2 87-101.

Cooper, C. (1996). *Conflict/Dispute Resolution Training & Police Officers.* Copenhagen, Denmark: University of Copenhagen, Sociologisk Institut.